"If there was ever a time for this ⟨...⟩ people are facing and what is about to happen ⟨...⟩ demands a generation that can pray. This book will help inspire and equip this end-times army of praying young history-makers. Read, and just do it."

LOU ENGLE, PRESIDENT AND FOUNDER OF
THE CALL AND ELIJAH REVOLUTION
AND AUTHOR OF *DIGGING THE WELLS OF REVIVAL*

"This book is full of inspirational stories and practical tools to encourage each reader that God is moving mightily among youth today. While many are pointing out obvious problems, Cheri Fuller and Ron Luce cast the spotlight on effective solutions and provide some of the most exhilarating stories of what happens *When Teens Pray*. Every parent, leader, and pastor should read this book and then pass it on to a teenager."

TOMMY BARNETT, PASTOR, PHOENIX FIRST ASSEMBLY OF GOD

"*When Teens Pray* is an awesome testimony of God's heart for this generation! It will inspire, encourage, and equip you to join Him in the adventure of prayer and give you a fresh vision for revival and awakening."

NANCY WILSON, ASSOCIATE NATIONAL DIRECTOR AND
INTERNATIONAL AMBASSADOR, STUDENT VENTURE

"It would be difficult to imagine a teenager *not* connecting with one of the true stories in *When Teens Pray*. They will. I envision God using this book to ignite a practical passion in the hearts of students and to challenge adults to believe that

God will use this generation as an instrument of awakening in our world. This book paints a wholly different picture of the "millennial" generation portrayed in the media. Truly, God is raising up an army of sold-out believers who are making a dynamic difference; in *When Teens Pray,* you'll hear *their* voices and read their stories."

DOUG CLARK, DIRECTOR OF FIELD MINISTRIES,
NATIONAL NETWORK OF YOUTH MINISTRIES

"*When Teens Pray* will inspire youth across our nation! Youth *are* praying, and the stories in this book prove they're getting real *answers* to and real *results* from their prayers. These great prayer strategies will show you how to join them—*today!*"

TOM SIPLING, JOSHUA JOURNEY MINISTRIES

"*When Teens Pray* captures the awesome movement of God being led by today's courageous, praying teens. Their stories, their faith, and their practical ideas for ongoing prayer make this book a must-read for teenagers, youth workers, and parents alike."

DOUG TEGNER, EXECUTIVE DIRECTOR, CAMPUS ALLIANCE

"You will be inspired and challenged to pray like never before as you read the true stories in this book!"

REBECCA ST. JAMES

when teens Pray

cheri Fuller
and RON LUCE

Multnomah Books

WHEN TEENS PRAY
published by Multnomah Books
A division of Random House, Inc.
and in association with the literary agency of Alive Communications, Inc.,
7680 Goddard Street, Suite 200, Colorado Springs, CO 80920

© 2002 by Cheri Fuller Communications, Inc., and Ron Luce
International Standard Book Number: 978-1-57673-970-9

Unless otherwise indicated, Scripture quotations are from:
The Holy Bible, New International Version
© 1973, 1984 by International Bible Society,
used by permission of Zondervan Publishing House
Other Scripture quotations:
The Living Bible (TLB)
© 1971. Used by permission of Tyndale House Publishers, Inc.
All rights reserved.
The Holy Bible, King James Version (KJV)
The Holy Bible, New King James Version (NKJV)
© 1984 by Thomas Nelson, Inc.
Holy Bible, New Living Translation (NLT)
© 1996. Used by permission of Tyndale House Publishers, Inc.
All rights reserved.

For information:
MULTNOMAH BOOKS • 12265 ORACLE BOULEVARD, SUITE 200
COLORADO SPRINGS, CO 80921
Library of Congress Cataloging-in-Publication Data:
Fuller, Cheri.
    When teens pray / by Cheri Fuller and Ron Luce.
        p.   cm.
    ISBN 1-57673-970-8 (pbk.)
    1. Christian teenagers—Religious life. 2. Prayer—Christianity.
I. Luce, Ron II. Title.
    BV4531.3 .F85 2002
248.3'2'0835—dc21   2002003745

08—10 9 8 7

CONTENTS

THANKS!

My heartfelt thanks to all the young people who shared their stories with us.[*] I'm standing on my tiptoes watching God work as your generation prays, and I'm joining in intercession—both with and for you!

Thanks to the Teen Mania team for the web page and to Julianne Klassen, Sarah Kotrba, Erin Dimeolo, and all the teen maniacs around the world who contributed their stories to the book. We also appreciate the focus group of teens who reviewed the manuscript.

Many thanks to Doug Clark of the National Network of Youth Ministries, Nancy Wilson of Student Venture, Doug Tegner of Campus Alliance, Tom Sipling of Joshua Journey Ministries, Keith Malcom of Campus Ministry Network, Mark Moder of Reach the Campus ministry, and the other terrific youth ministry workers and specialists who shared stories and helped connect us with teens who are impacting their campuses and communities.

I am grateful to my insightful, gracious editors, Judith St. Pierre and Jennifer Gott, and to Don Jacobson and Multnomah Publishers for their strong belief in the power of prayer and for sharing my vision for the When We Pray series.

I also want to acknowledge the intercession of Moms In Touch International, which was founded by Fern Nichols in the very year that prayer was taken out of U.S. schools and ever since has been praying for elementary, junior high, and high schools and this generation of young people. I've found that as we pray for our children and youth, they rise up as intercessors for their generation—and that's exactly what has happened, as you'll read in the pages ahead.

Thanks to Greg Johnson for his support and friendship and to David Ryle for his editorial help early in the project. And to Peggy Stewart, friend and prayer partner, who came alongside at just the right moment; and Melanie Hemry, for all you contributed, thanks from the bottom of my heart!

I am always grateful for my husband, Holmes, and ever thankful as he joins me in responding to the call God is issuing—for all of us to pray!

Cheri Fuller

[*]In a few cases the names of teens have been changed to protect their privacy.

WHY READ THiS BOOK?

Because the stories you're about to read could absolutely change your life!

In these stories you'll see what happens when young people take God at His word and have the courage to believe that He will answer their prayers. You'll see, over and over again, the kind of miracles and amazing changes that happen when teens pray. The fact is that God wants to do great things through you and for you—He's just waiting for you to ask.

Here are the powerful stories of teens who did ask...and then watched God move on their behalf. We hope that their experiences encourage you to fall on your knees and press into the presence of God for yourself. We hope that your prayer life will become much more than the ritual of praying through a prayer list or just something you do before your meal or during a church service. We hope that it will become an intimate time when you rendezvous with God each day to pray for specific needs, a time when you ask God to move in huge ways in your school, in your home, and in the world. We hope for all these things because when teens pray and really connect with God, the world is never the same...and neither are they.

Even before the terrorist attacks on September 11, 2001, there was a growing river of prayer among youth, but in the wake of this national tragedy, thousands of teens have gone to war—on their knees. God is raising up a new generation of young people who are seriously seeking Him. Unprecedented numbers of youth are meeting at their flagpoles to pray, prayer-walking their campuses, and fasting and praying for revival in their high schools, families, nation, and world. And, as you'll see in the pages ahead, the result is that many are being set free from suicide, abuse, addictions, and other bondages as they lift up their prayers to God. God is on a search and rescue mission, and He is calling your generation to seek Him as never before! That's what this book is about.

We've designed it so you can go directly to the section that will best connect with your needs right now. For example, if you're feeling desperate, start with chapter 12. If you're worried about a friend or struggle in your faith, chapters 2 and 14 are where to begin. If you want God to move in your school or if you're about to give up or if you're praying alone...whatever your situation, this book is designed especially for you.

You'll also find power points called "God Links" throughout. These prayer strategies, creative ideas, and web sites will help you connect with God, pray more effectively, and be set on fire for God. And in the last part of the book are pages for you to write your own prayer needs and requests and journal about how God answers as you pray.

Our prayer is that as you read this book and begin your own adventure in prayer—and get others to join you—you'll discover the amazing ways God works...when teens pray!

1

iF GOD HAS GIVEN YOU A VISION...

Extraordinary prayer ignites the flame. A great movement of God's Spirit is always preceded by beyond-the-norm prayer. And prayer is the fuse that's been lit among today's youth, consuming their generation as it moves through.

Barry St. Clair

The Tidal Wave

From the time I was a kid, I played all kinds of sports, but my favorite was ice hockey. The summer before my junior year, I had a chance to attend a boarding school in Casper, Wyoming, to play hockey, a stepping-stone to a college hockey scholarship and a pro career. I had to choose: Should I go to school in Wyoming or stay at Mays High School in Wichita, Kansas? Since my parents said they'd support whatever I decided, I realized that I had to ask God and listen for His direction.

One day while I was talking to God about the decision, I heard Him say, "You can serve Me now as a young man or later as an older man. But one day, son, you'll serve Me full time." That settled it. I'd stay in my high school and pursue God and His purpose there instead of a hockey career.

I caught the desire to pray for my high school when I attended a prayer conference with my family. I watched as two thousand people moved from banner to banner, praying for nations, for America, and for the lost. Back home after that conference, I read about the lives of some famous Christians like Charles Finney, John Wesley, and John G. Lake. The lives of these three men inspired me so much that I began praying an hour before school each morning.

One morning while I prayed alone in my room, my eyes opened to a startling sight. I saw the North American continent covered in wheat—ready for harvest. Instantly, I found myself standing in the middle of the United States, facing the East Coast. As I watched this vision, a black wave hundreds of miles wide crested and moved quickly inland so that it blocked out the light of day.

Sheer terror gripped me, and I turned toward the west. I saw another wave of clear blue water heading toward me from the western seaboard. The two waves collided in the Midwest, and the western wave engulfed the black wave from the East Coast.

Seconds later, the vision ended.

The Lord explained to me that although darkness is sweeping our nation in a tidal wave of wickedness, God is sending a wave of His power to shake this generation. In this vision, I saw four major prayer needs:

1. salvation of the lost in my school,
2. spiritual warfare to break the strongholds of suicide, violence, drugs, and other addictions,
3 my school's leadership,
4. a move of God to bring spiritual awakening and revival.

I shared these things with the Christian club at my school, but the other members thought praying for the lost as a group sounded like a crazy idea. So, for weeks nobody joined me as I prayed. Finally, my cousin and a few friends agreed to pray.

The principal gave us permission to meet in the Spanish room once a week before school. I made four brightly colored banners, each representing one of the four prayer needs. Every Tuesday at 7 A.M. we propped the banners against the wall and wrote the names of individual students and teachers on them. Then, spending five minutes at each banner, we prayed for each by name.

Next, the Lord impressed on us to anoint the doorposts of the school with oil every Friday morning and pray that everyone who passed through the doorways would come under the blood covering of Christ. We also prayed that whatever bondage or hindrance was keeping them from God would be overcome and their hearts would be open to the Holy Spirit.

Then God taught us about fasting. It seemed like every time I opened the Bible, I saw references to fasting. After reading about Daniel's fast, our group began a twenty-one-day fast. We divided the time into increments of three or more days so everyone would feel able to participate and so someone would be fasting at all times. After the fast, things changed. Before we fasted, we'd been praying, *God give us our school! Please give us our school!*

When we finished the fast, God told us to stop praying that prayer—because the jurisdiction of the school was *ours*.

From then on, the Holy Spirit went to work. One pom-pom girl, alone in her room, suddenly realized that she needed Jesus. She found one of the girls in our prayer group to talk with and gave her life to the Lord.

One hall of the school was dominated by the occult, with a strong Wiccan influence pervading the group. But when one of the girls came to me and asked for prayer, the entire hall changed. Even in class, students asked for prayer and gave their lives to the Lord. God delivered teens from drug addictions. Apathetic Christians suddenly hungered for more of God. Our early-morning prayer group grew from a few students to twenty...then thirty...and more.

Two years after I graduated from high school, one of the wildest boys in school, whom we'd prayed for, was radically saved. Within a month his mother and sister gave their lives to the Lord as well.

I believe that God is calling teenagers to rise up and defeat the wave of darkness that threatens this nation. We can take this generation for God!

Brandon Page

GOD LINKS

Because of Brandon's choice to pursue God and lead his high school in prayer, not only did God move on his campus, the tidal wave spread to many others as he shared the vision and equipped teens to pray until almost every middle, junior high, and high school in his area of Kansas had an active group of intercessors praying for God's Spirit to move at their school. Here's how to use this effective prayer strategy.

Using cardboard or sheets of paper, make four banners that describe the theme of each station. These four prayer targets will help you focus your prayers to transform your school. Then divide into small groups and have each group move from station to station, praying until all are covered:

Station 1. Pray that God will save the lost. (2 Peter 3:9)
Ask God to intervene and save your lost classmates.

Station 2. Pray that God will move in the lives of teachers and administration. (1 Timothy 2:1-2)
Part of our responsibility as Christians is to pray that God's blessing will rest on those in positions of authority.

Station 3. Pray that God will break strongholds in your school through spiritual warfare. (2 Corinthians 10:4)
It's important to ask God to show you where Satan has control in your school. When you can identify the strongholds, you can then pray that God will break them and move feely in your school.

Station 4. Pray that God will send revival. (Acts 2:17)
If you will pray, God will send a revival and not just thousands but millions of young people will be saved.

(Adapted from *OneTwenty Prayer Manual* by Brandon Page and Terry Johnson. For more information, you can send an e-mail to onetwenty3768@yahoo.com.)

aftershock

I was the son of a pastor and born into a Christian family—becoming a Christian should have been no problem for me, right? *Wrong!* At age seventeen, my heart was as hard as granite. I felt bitter toward God and believed that He had betrayed me. And I thought my father was foolish for leaving a lucrative family business to become a pastor. So I ran from God. I stated openly that I didn't want to serve Him, and my life began to spin out of control. I got high, sold drugs, and lived the thug life.

But my mother cried out to God in prayer. As head of the prayer band at the church, she put my name on a "hit list" before God and rallied others to pray for me too. Although I seemed to only get worse, she prayed and fasted for me consistently and never gave up.

Finally this prodigal son came home to the Father's heart. My life as a thug and drug dealer ended abruptly when I was born again in 1996. A few months later, I walked up to the church I attended, Christ Tabernacle, and saw that the surrounding neighborhoods were controlled by gangs, drugs, and violence. At night, long lines of people waited to get into the clubs, yet most teenagers never even noticed the nearby church.

One morning as I was vacuuming the church and singing to the Lord, God dropped two words in my heart: *Youth Explosion.* As clearly as I saw the vacuum cleaner in my hand, I saw thousands of youth lining up to get into the church and give their hearts to Jesus.

The image I got was of a concert-style event designed to attract teens. I took the idea to the pastors at Christ Tabernacle, and they agreed to pursue the concept. I had joined a Friday night prayer group, and we began praying and fasting for the event and the teens who would be attending—just as my mother had done for me.

The first Youth Explosion meeting was scheduled for November 1996. I heard comments like, "They'll be lucky if a few show up...." As disheartening as those comments were, I knew that *luck* would have nothing to do with it. Either God would bless it with His presence or He wouldn't.

I firmly believed that He would show up.

The night of that first meeting, the sanctuary held a packed crowd with standing room only. Sixty teens gave their lives to the Lord. Afterward, we prayed like we'd never prayed before for God to transform the lives of people in our community. We also held Bible studies on Friday nights that were divided into two groups: one for senior high and one for junior high students. The Bible study began with only eighteen people—most still preferring the dances held at the YMCA or at some other club. But by December 1997, as a result of fasting and prayer, one hundred youth were attending. The two groups combined into one meeting called "Aftershock."

Four times in 1997 we held Youth Explosions, and each time God showed up in a powerful way to those who packed into the building. After eighteen months the Aftershock meetings had outgrown the fellowship hall and moved to the church sanctuary. By April 2001, around five hundred youth were participating in these meetings. The Aftershock meetings were every Friday night, the Youth Explosions scheduled periodically.

Every Friday a prayer band of teenagers fasted all day and met from 5:30 to 7:00 P.M. to pray for the evening's Aftershock. At 7:00, two hundred of the core group gathered at the altar to call upon the Lord as a line formed outside. No one could miss the fact that this line was forming around the block of a church with a cross rather than at a club.

We placed a three-by-four-foot Plexiglas box on the platform to hold the things the Holy Spirit convicted people to give up. We never suggested that kids give up their stuff, but we learned quickly that the Holy Spirit would convict them. One girl threw in a stack of letters from an ungodly relationship. A drug dealer threw in several hundred dollars worth of marijuana. Box cutters, knives, gang colors, and secular CDs appeared in the box weekly, remnants of old lifestyles young people tossed aside as they turned to Christ.

One night, two rival gangs came to Aftershock. One gang had brought along knives to slash the other group with. While music played before the meeting, a gang member who was over six feet tall walked up to a much shorter usher. With tears in his eyes he said, "I don't know what's in this place, but we can't do this." He handed the usher his knives. After the meeting the whole gang gave their hearts to Jesus.

By the end of 2001 the box was so full and so heavy that

it was cracking. It weighed over six hundred pounds! We had to bring in a new box.

And as the Aftershock meetings grew, the director of the YMCA, who was not a Christian, became curious about his competition and came to one of the meetings. He began to cry during the service and later stood up and said that he was going to shut down the dance. Truthfully, once God shows up, any teenager would rather be in His presence than at a dance. The world just can't compete with God.

Aftershock is now the largest youth group in New York City. At the first meeting of 2002, almost one thousand young people lined up to get inside. Gone are the days when the church hunkers down just to survive the crime in the city. We are now what God always intended us to be—a beacon of light in the darkness. And as the pastor of Youth Explosion Ministries, I continue in prayer and fasting, depending completely on God.

Together with my wife, Luz, and the young people we work with, we continue to petition the Lord for more souls among this generation and believe that He will provide even greater things.

This is my prayer for every teen reading this book:

May God reveal to you the great and awesome plan He has for your life. May you and all your generation climb from under the rubble of sin and ascend to your destiny. May you wash your hands and your hearts in the blood of the Lamb, allowing Him to cleanse both your actions and the motives of your heart. May every man-made idol in your life turn to dust. May you never again be captivated by MTV stars, by the drug dealer on the corner, by the music industry, or by this world's standards. May you, like the psalmist David, cry out to God, "Whom have I in heaven but you? And earth has nothing I desire besides you" (Psalm 73:25). And above all, may you answer the great and glorious call to pray.

Pastor Adam Durso
For more information,
visit www.youthexplosion.com.

GOD LINKS

When you go to war on your knees by battling in prayer, you will meet some opposition from the enemy. You need a prayer shield much like Adam's mom provided.

Find some praying moms and grandmas.

Connect with local Moms In Touch groups and ask them to pray for protection, guidance, and impact. Also ask dads, neighbors, and friends to pray.

Plug in to your church's prayer ministry.

Let the senior pastor, youth pastor, and prayer ministry coordinators at your church know about your prayer needs, and ask them to pray for your group on an ongoing basis. If your church has a prayer chain or prayer chapel with twenty-four-hour coverage, write out your group's regular prayer needs and give them to the intercessors. Update prayer needs and testimonies about what God is doing weekly.

Get in to a network.

It's great to get involved in a citywide network of youth ministries that can encourage, equip, and pray. Campus Ministry Network in the Wichita, Kansas, area has a newsletter and web site, holds training sessions for students wanting to lead campus Bible studies and prayer groups, and enlists "Partners in Prayer" to pray for the teens and schools in their community. By networking and praying together, they are seeing revival on every campus in the county. (Contact Keith Malcom at 316-773-4444 for information.)

Unite.

You don't have to stand alone! Join with other high school prayer groups in your area to start an Internet site, do an outreach together, or pray for one another. Join Prayer Challenge, which encourages and equips churches and groups to cover every school in America in prayer. For more information, go to www.prayerchallenge.com.

Living proof

I stood on the large, grassy Mall in Washington, D.C., along with four hundred thousand other people who were fasting and praying for our nation, our families, and our generation during The Call D.C. Thousands of teens, little kids, and parents were there. The crowd, standing shoulder to shoulder, included people of every race and denomination.

At 3:00 P.M. we were urged to pray for our families. Just then I felt as though a supernatural switch went off in my spirit. In my mind's eye, I saw my thirteen-year-old brother's name flashing like a neon sign.

Charles…Charles…Charles…

I knew instinctively that something was wrong—dead wrong.

My whole body shook, and I dropped to my knees in the grass, weeping. Charles hadn't committed his life to Jesus, but I knew somehow that it wasn't just his salvation I was pleading for. It felt like I was fighting for my brother's life. I could almost see a spirit of death hovering over him, and I knew that the only thing holding it back was my prayer.

"Lord, guard and protect Charles," I prayed. "Have mercy on him right now, Father! He needs You!" While I prayed, it seemed as though all of heaven wept with me. As we prayed, a heavy rain began to pour. My face, buried in the ground, was covered with mud, but I hardly noticed. I didn't care about anything or anyone except Charles. I wasn't even aware of the people crowding around me, and although the stage with the prayer leaders was only fifty yards away, I was oblivious. After a while, I began to realize that people everywhere were weeping as they prayed for their families.

For thirty minutes I prayed intensely—then as suddenly as the burden came, it lifted. I sat up and looked around, then joined the group for the remainder of the corporate prayer.

I arrived back in Dallas a few days later and phoned my parents in Atlanta.

"How's everything at home?" I asked Mom.

"Something happened to Charles," she said. "I'll let him tell you about it."

Charles took the phone and described the day I'd been in Washington, D.C., praying. He'd been riding his motorcycle in the mountains with Dad and had gone ahead, when he approached a blind turn. The turn dropped off to a sheer cliff from which many bikers had fallen to their deaths. At 3:00 that afternoon, his rear tire slipped—plunging him into a 150-yard free fall.

That should have been the end of it: my thirteen-year-old brother dead at the scene. But at 3:25 some other bikers discovered him—alive. He suffered a few scratches, but no broken bones.

Although I'd prayed for years, I never understood the *reality* of the power of prayer until that day at the Washington, D.C., Mall.

My brother is living proof.

Alyssa Broom

GOD LINKS

call gatherings

The Call New England gathered together thousands of teens only eleven days after the terrorist attacks, on September 22, 2002. Call gatherings are being planned for New York City, Dallas, Hollywood, Brazil, and England, to dig deeper the wells of revival and to pray that America will turn to God.

Visit www.thecallrevolution.com

for more information.

standoff at western High

Western High School was not a safe place for students or teachers when the school year began in 2000. Anger simmered just beneath the surface in every class, in the library, in the cafeteria, and in the parking lot. Fights erupted frequently. Even the teachers lived in fear because of death threats. Students and teachers alike kept their heads down and hoped to be out of range when tempers flared.

Bullies and hotheads ruled the school, but witches also had a strong presence, and the Muslim club boasted a healthy membership. But the Bible club was the smallest on campus—only four members.

There didn't seem to be much the students, faculty, or school board could do to change the atmosphere at Western. It seemed like just another symptom of a troubled society.

Like everyone else, Tayo Ikotun saw no solution to the escalating problems at Western High until she heard Tom Sipling issue a challenge at a youth group meeting. He urged students to take a stand for Christ by praying the 30 Second Kneel Down (30KD) at their school sometime each day.

Tayo couldn't take this challenge lightly. It meant she might be made fun of or draw attention to herself in an already heated environment. If she did this and God didn't arrive on the scene and intervene, things could get much worse—especially for her.

But what if God does hear my prayer and intervene? she thought. Would the outcome be worth the risk? Would it be worth her reputation? Worth being the source of jokes?

The night before the new school year began, Tayo saw a mental picture of herself and her friend Patricia dancing at school as a way to worship God. Tayo shivered when she talked to Patricia and learned that God had given her the same idea.

On the first day of school, both girls rushed through the halls to find their classes. But after school, with dry mouths and clammy hands, they met in the foyer and danced to the song "Shackles." Everyone moved out of the way, not wanting to be associated with anything weird. Most kids didn't have any idea what the girls were doing or why. Many just looked, shrugged, and then walked away.

Nothing visible happened to the school or the student body after their dancing, but something amazing happened to Tayo and Patricia. Although the school may not have broken free, the girls did. Fear left Tayo and Patricia, and they felt overwhelmed by a sense of peace.

And they needed that peace for the next step of obedience: the 30 Second Kneel Down—a demonstration of their beliefs that no one would misunderstand.

The following morning, the hall at their school was filled with sounds of chatter, book bags dropping, and lockers slamming. A few friends laughed and visited. Other kids seemed depressed or angry.

Tayo and Patricia took a deep breath and kneeled on the floor in front of their lockers. No one paid much attention. They bowed their heads and prayed silently. Thirty seconds seemed like an eternity.

Then some people began to notice.

"What are they doing?"

"I think they're praying."

"What a couple of freaks!"

Finally, Tayo and Patricia stood, gathered their books, and went to class. *We did it!* Tayo thought. *We made our stand.*

Every day for a week, they kneeled and prayed for their school, classmates, and teachers—the thirty seconds stretching into more. Tayo went to the Bible club and explained the concept to them.

"Don't do this because it's some kind of trend or a nice thing to do," she said. "Go home and pray. Ask God to give you conviction about it so that you'll do it from your heart with the right motive."

Soon, others joined them.

But their silent prayers enraged a group of witches who protested that the Christians' kneeling and praying violated their constitutional rights. Although the pray-ers were within their rights to pray silently, the witches claimed that the Christians' actions were a way of pushing their religion on them, and a controversy arose. The witches wrote slanderous statements and curses on the bathroom walls. Tayo and her Christian friends moved their prayer near the witches' lockers, who reacted by screaming and cursing them.

But the persecution against the Christian students had an amazing result: Other students joined them. The Bible club grew until it was the largest club at Western High, even surpassing the Muslim club.

For the first time in years, the fighting stopped. The teachers received no death threats. One teacher who had taught at the school for fifteen years said, "This is the first year I've ever had a peaceful homeroom. I wasn't threatened. Students didn't disrupt class and were actually interested in learning."

The God of all glory inclined His ear to the teens that invited Him to their school. The Creator of the universe, who hung the sun and moon in place and created the earth and all its fullness, showed up at Western High.

GOD LINKS

the 30 second kneel down

30KD is a prayer evangelism strategy for middle and high school campuses. At school at 7:30 A.M., or at any time during the school day, take thirty seconds to pray like this:

SEGMENT 1

God, thanks! (see Matthew 22:37)

God, I bow my knee in humility to You. I know that Your loving presence will be with me all day. Thank You for loving me today. I love You, too!

SEGMENT 2

God, touch them! (see Matthew 22:39)

God, touch the teachers, administration, and students on my campus today. One touch from You, Father, can change someone's destiny. Touch them through me.

SEGMENT 3

God, tell them! (see Matthew 28:19)

God, the message of Jesus' love for my campus must be told. Use me as the messenger. I will tell those around me how much You love them.

(For more information from Joshua Journey Ministries, go to 30kd.org.)

if YOU'RE PRAYING FOR YOUR FRIENDS...

Praying is simply a two-way conversation
between you and God....
Prayer is not our using of God;
it more often puts us in a position
where God can use us.

Billy Graham

Anything's possible

You'd think that praying for one of your friends wouldn't be such a difficult assignment—right? But what if that friend doesn't even want to change and nothing ever seems to happen as a result of your prayers?

As a freshman, Daniel King was challenged during Club 121 (the campus Christian group) to pray for his friends and his school. Daniel chose to pray for his friend Tommy, a popular guy everybody loved.

Every year the Homecoming Prince, Tommy was good looking and a class leader. He had the girls' attention. He had people looking up to him. He had everything. Everything that is, but one thing: He didn't know God. Part of the partying crowd, Tommy was a big drinker, and he and his family weren't churchgoers. Once in a while he'd go along with Daniel to a youth event just because they were friends, but he didn't budge spiritually.

Daniel prayed for months, and then a year and another. But nothing seemed to be happening. His prayers every day for Tommy became monotonous. And there was nothing to show for his efforts. Tommy still partied and drank and had no interest in God. But the boys remained close friends, and a still, small voice kept reminding Daniel to hang in there and persevere in prayer for Tommy, for his school, and for other unsaved friends. Three years passed.

It wasn't until right before Daniel's senior year that God answered his prayers. He had just gotten back from a mission trip to Hungary and Romania and then went straight to youth camp to serve as a counselor.

As Daniel walked into the main pavilion, who should he run into but Tommy!

But something was different—he could see it in his friend's eyes even before Tommy began to tell him how he'd given his life to Christ while Daniel was out of the country. Tommy had done a 180-degree turnaround and now was a cabin leader at the Christian camp.

Five more of Daniel's friends fell like dominoes that summer—right into the arms of Jesus. Fueled with faith at seeing what God had done in Tommy's life and in the lives of his other friends, Daniel went back to school and reached out to other students and soon brought some of the hardcore partyers in his high school to Christ.

Then he called together sixty Christian friends, including the new believers, to pray over every building and room on campus, over the entire student body, and over the football field of Blue Springs High School. The next day when the doors opened for the first day of school, it was obvious that God was on the move. At their first Club 121 meeting, a record 180 students showed up. Kids from all different denominations got out of their comfort zones and cliques with one goal in mind: to reach their campus for Jesus Christ.

When Daniel graduated, he left behind a much stronger, larger group of believers than when he'd begun as a freshman—teens who would continue to see God move mountains and turn their school and city upside down. Opportunities opened up for Daniel to speak to youth around the nation, encouraging them never to give up praying for their high schools and friends. "Through it all I learned we don't know God's timing or understand the plan He has, but we're to ask, seek, knock, and not stop praying for our friends," says Daniel. With a little faith—mixed with sincere prayer—anything is possible.

GOD LINKS

When you're praying for people long-term, as Daniel did for Tommy, here's a practical way to use the word **BLESS** to break things down and keep your prayers from becoming monotonous:

Body
Pray for their physical health, protection, and safety.

Labor
Pray blessings on their studies or jobs.

Emotional
Pray for their emotional life, especially that they can trust God and experience joy, peace, and hope instead of worry, fear, loneliness, and insecurity.

Social
Pray blessings on their relationships with their family and friends.

Spiritual
Pray that they will experience the greatest blessing of all—knowing Christ and experiencing His grace and salvation.

(Adapted from H.O.P.E.'s booklet *Make Your Home a Power House*.)

one Broken Life

I attended a winter retreat with my youth group. And during the worship one day I felt so drawn to the Lord that I said, "You can have all of me. You can have all my hopes and dreams." I thought that was a pretty big commitment and maybe—someday when I was older—God would call me to Africa or India.

I never expected Him to call me to a far scarier place—right now, right where I lived.

But God spoke to me that weekend, and His voice echoed through every cell of my being. *I want you to reach twenty friends for Jesus before the end of your sophomore year.*

Twenty!

I returned home from the retreat and took the 6 A.M. time in a youth prayer chain at my church. Each morning I woke early and prayed for the students at my school. A few months later, I heard that the play *Heaven's Gates, Hell's Flames* was coming to my church. So I took a deep breath and began inviting a few of the friends I'd been praying for. Then I invited a few more. The weekend before the performance I called fifty students to invite them to the play. And I also invited fifteen of my closest friends.

When one of the cast members gave an invitation after the play, all fifteen of my close friends gave their hearts and lives to Jesus. The next night I took ten teens with me to the play. All ten accepted Jesus as their Lord and Savior.

God gave me!

of the play left, God nudged me to
"—the cheerleaders, football play-
party group from school.

of me? I wondered. But I forced
vited them. Twenty attended the
of the performance, the captain
down the aisle to accept Christ.

ad touched forty-five teenagers!
other Christians in prayer at See
. I decorated invitations with flag stickers and
them on the new believers' lockers. None of them had
ever attended a prayer gathering, but on the third
Wednesday in September *all forty-five* showed up at the flagpole to pray for our school.

"What are you doing here?" some of the Christians
asked one guy who'd been known for using God's name as
a curse word. "I accepted Jesus, and I'm praying for this
school!" he announced. He stood beside a former drug user,
a cheerleader, and some football players. In all, 130 teens
prayed that day.

That day reminded me of the way Jesus took some fish
and a few loaves of bread and multiplied them to feed thousands of people. I've learned that He's still in the business of
miracle multiplication.

All He needs is one broken life.

Stacy Hanson

Hanging Out with GOD

GOD LINKS

One of Jesus' most awesome moments in prayer happened when He took His disciples up to the Mount of Transfiguration to pray (read the story in Luke 9:28–36). While they were praying, Elijah and Moses showed up. They started hanging out and talking, and suddenly the presence of God came. God began to speak audibly, and Jesus began to glow!

Now, there is no indication in Scripture that they believed this prayer time was going to be different than any other. Jesus was just going to spend time with His Father and pray as He often did…yet they encountered the glory of God. So can you! Imagine the kind of quiet times you can have with God—hanging out, getting intimate, and listening to His voice.

Remind yourself daily that meeting with God is more important than it would be to meet with the President of the United States…or anyone else. Allow God to transform your mind, your heart, and your attitude so you become more like Him every day and continually bring His light to the world. If you do these things, you can become a world-changer, because you have met in secret with God and received His power in your life each day.

3 iF YOU'RE ON THE MISSION FIELD...

Prayer is the walkie-talkie on the battlefield of the world.

John Piper

A face in the crowd

In the summer of 2000, I was all geared up for a mission trip to Haiti, but due to political unrest my team ended up going to Panama instead. As I rode through the streets of Panama City, I prayed for God to show me someone He wanted me to reach. I'd no sooner asked God for that than a man's face appeared in my mind. He was a brown-skinned Indian with a thin mustache. When he smiled, I saw that he was missing a bottom tooth.

I tucked the memory of the man's face in my heart and began to pray for him every day. *Lord, start now to soften his heart,* I prayed. *Prepare him to hear the message of the gospel.*

Help me to say or do whatever You want me to.

As we traveled through Panama City, I scanned the crowds of people for the familiar face from my mind's eye, but I didn't see anyone with a mustache. I learned that most of the Indian men didn't have enough facial hair to grow a mustache. So who was the man I'd seen?

After four days of ministering in Panama City, we headed to the Darien Jungle to visit a tribe of Cuna Indians. We arrived at the village of Peria with some apprehension because the villagers had kicked out the last team that attempted to minister there.

The Teen Mania team leaders first had to go to the chief and ask permission for us to stay a few days. Then the men had to meet at the Congress House, where the other village leaders and the rest of the villagers would make a decision. Because of how they had treated other missionaries, we were afraid that the people in the village didn't want us there and didn't want to hear anything we had to say.

However, the chief told us that we could stay—under certain conditions. First, we had to stay in a particular hut with a translator. We also had to pay a sum of money.

It was late in the afternoon before I finally got to go inside and meet the chief. When I saw him, I thought my heart would stop. *It was him!* The chief gazed at me from a familiar face. He had a pencil-thin mustache, and when he smiled, I saw the missing tooth.

God, what are You doing? He's the chief of a tribe that doesn't want us here!

Later, while the chief was at the Congress House, we

circled his empty stool and prayed for him. Moments later he walked in and sat down—and looked right at me. We couldn't understand each other's language, but somehow in that instant we connected.

Two days later the ministry team performed a drama called "The Journey" for the village. It tells the story of how all people search for their Creator and try to understand their purpose on earth. The chief and others crowded around to watch. But after the presentation, not one person accepted Jesus.

My heart thumping in my chest, I grabbed Jose, the interpreter, and approached the chief. "God told me to come to your village and give you a message," I said. "He told me to tell you that He created the wood you worship as your god. He wants you to turn from those other gods and worship Him alone. Would you like to know how you can receive the one true God?"

Even before Jose finished translating, the chief nodded his head, tears glistening in his eyes. I led him to Jesus; then Jose gave his life to the Lord as well.

Later that night the team performed the drama for the last time, teens and children packing the hut. Then the chief and Jose told all the villagers that the two of them had accepted Jesus as their Savior. Most of the people weren't ready to give up their spirit gods, but I felt blessed to know that God now had an opening in the village.

Since our visit, mission teams are readily accepted in the village, and there is a vacation Bible school in the village with a growing number of believers.

Dan Barnett

GOD LINKS

Teen Mania's Global Expeditions

Have you been praying for God to move in your nation and other nations around the world? How would you like to see God answer your prayers face-to-face?

Every summer thousands of teens join Teen Mania's Global Expeditions for life-changing adventures to over thirty different locations around the world. By taking the challenge to change your world by going on a mission trip, you will be able to have a firsthand experience just like the stories you have heard in this book.

With Teen Mania you will have the opportunity to go on a two-week, one-month, or two-month mission trip. You can even bring your youth group along.

If you want more information about Teen Mania's Global Expeditions, check out www.globalexpeditions.com or call 1-866-5-GLOBEX.

Amsterdam Answers

I had never been on a different continent than my parents, so flying across the Atlantic to Europe was enough to make me nervous. Our mission field was the red-light district of Amsterdam. We were naïve teenagers who had never been exposed to something so blatant as women soliciting strangers on the street. Some drugs are also legal in the Netherlands. Drugs, pornography, and prostitution are woven into certain facets of the society—and were very prevalent in the area of Amsterdam where we would be ministering.

And that's what really made me nervous. We were too young and naïve for this place—we would probably be so overwhelmed by what we saw that we wouldn't know what to do. How would we ever make a difference in anyone's life here?

I shared my concerns with the group as we walked down a street in the city and found out that others felt the same way. We stopped walking and prayed for divine intervention. Then we continued on and someone began to hum. Soon we were in the middle of a full-blown worship session.

Then it happened.

We saw a group of homeless teenagers on the street corner, their vacant stares telling stories we would never know. Emboldened by our prayers, we stopped and shared our faith with the group. But they quickly rejected us and our message.

I turned around as we were about to leave. "If one thing would help you believe in God, what would it be?"

"To have a full stomach immediately," one teen replied.

We prayed, calling on God as Jehovah-jireh—our provider—and asked for food to fill the teens' stomachs. We claimed God's promise that He cares for the birds and that He would care even more for His children.

We'd no sooner said "Amen" than a man walked up to us carrying a huge garbage bag. "I just walked by a bakery, and they were about to throw out their doughnuts because they're going to make fresh ones in the morning. You guys want them?"

Doughnuts! Empty stares came alive with excitement. I don't know how long it'd been since those teens had had the luxury of a doughnut, but not so much as a crumb was left when they finished. Then, with full bellies, they asked about Jesus. Later, after discussion and prayer, several of the teens gave their lives to the Lord.

There had been a hole in my theory about what God could do in the red-light district of Amsterdam. But God showed me that just as He used a few loaves of bread and some fish to feed the multitudes in the Bible, He could use some doughnuts to bring the Bread of Life to a group of hungry Dutch teens that day.

Lily Kim

GOD LINKS

Whether your mission field is the inner city of your town or a faraway country, here are some tips on prayer-walking. Divide into small groups and then:

Keep your eyes wide open...
Before you pray, take time to observe what is happening, what the particular area you're in is like, and what the needs of the people are.

Observe specifics...
Like people's customs, dress, physical needs, and religious beliefs.

Use the knowledge...
You've acquired through observation to pray specifically as God's Spirit prompts you. Talk to God about what you see and feel, and be sensitive to His guidance. Ask the Lord to show you what's on His heart for the people, and take time at the end to meet and share and thank God together.

No matter how extreme the needs in the area, know that your prayers *are* making a difference!

Deep in the Darien Jungle

The sounds of squawking birds and the rhythmic slapping of water against the canoe that was taking them deeper into the Darien Jungle of Panama reminded Jonathan Baldwin that, with every stroke of the oar, he was getting farther from home—and farther from his comfort zone. Before leaving on this trip with Teen Mania in the summer of 2000, Jonathan had read a book by John G. Lake, a missionary to Africa. Lake had experienced miracles and the supernatural manifestations of God to a degree that few people on earth had ever known. Challenged by the book, Jonathan had prepared for this trip with bold prayers and expectations of the supernatural.

Now, faced with towering trees and the reality of jungle life, Jonathan knew that he was no John G. Lake. He was just a teenager in the middle of a big jungle, well aware that without a big God he was in trouble. Jonathan rehearsed all the instructions his team leader had given. "Do *not* spill water in the huts!" he'd warned. "And don't step anywhere near their sacred tent. And don't do anything that would offend the villagers."

They dragged their canoes to the shore and trekked to the village. There they saw a man with a gaping wound on his hand. The skin around the cut had turned a dark color, and he couldn't move his hand. Jonathan's team gathered around to pray.

Pour water on the wound. The Lord spoke in a still, quiet voice.

But I can't act like some crazy teenager spilling water! Jonathan argued quietly. For twenty minutes he refused to obey God's command. Finally he prayed silently, *Lord, if You want me to pour water on his hand, confirm it by telling someone else.*

You know My voice! Do what I am telling you to do.

Jonathan slipped away to his backpack and got water, then asked his team leader for permission to pour water on the man's wound. Still hesitating, Jonathan finally poured water over the man's hand. Another team member began rubbing the man's hand. As she did, the skin around the wound changed to a normal color. They finished praying and watched as God healed the wound before their eyes. Moments later, the man moved his hand freely.

Seeing what God had done, Jonathan's team prayed in faith for more and bigger things. Within a few days many villagers experienced the greatest miracle of all: the resurrection of their spirit by the Spirit of God as they made Jesus the Lord of their lives.

4 if YOU NEED TO HEAR FROM GOD...

> If you want to know God,
> there is only one way to do it:
> Get down on your knees.
>
> Fulton J. Sheen

The Darkness of Despair

Charlie Hall was in trouble. Rebelling against his parents and estranged from his friends, Charlie sank into a dark depression. By the time he reached seventeen, it didn't seem like things could get any worse—but drinking, driving, and a car wreck proved him wrong. He was in trouble with his parents, in his relationships, and with the law. At the bottom of a pit of loneliness and despair, Charlie began searching for a way out.

"If God was really there, I didn't want to go halfway," Charlie explains. "If He was there, I would be willing to give myself to Him fully. But for me, that was a big *if*.

"I figured that if He was there, He would show himself to me if I asked. So I called out to God and asked Him to reveal

Himself. Nothing happened. There were no bright lights or voices. I went on dealing with things the best I could. Not too long after that, I was playing my guitar and fooling around with lyrics. I wasn't singing to God; I was just...singing."

The words Charlie sang were, "If I had my life to do all over again, I'd live it all for you." While he sang, the indescribable power and presence of God filled the room. It wrapped itself around Charlie as peace filled every hurting corner of his heart. Charlie's questions about God's existence fled, and he gave himself to the Creator.

"I knew immediately that I was called to pastor," Charlie says, "but I just couldn't see myself in a traditional role, wearing a coat and tie and working at a church. But God said, *I'm going to use you the way I made you—through song and music.*"

When Charlie experienced the reality of the living God, his whole outlook on life changed. "I had a huge desire to know the Lord and live for Him. I no longer wanted to drink and rebel. Over the next decade, my faith developed into a genuine passion for Jesus and a desire to see revival in America—especially in my generation."

After praying for ten years and working with youth, God allowed Charlie to lead worship for a group of between forty and fifty thousand young people that had gathered in a solemn assembly to devote themselves to God and pray for their generation. Since then, Charlie has released a number of CDs. Through his music, worship, and prayer, Charlie leads countless others out of the darkness of despair.

That prayer—that cry to God to reveal Himself—all those years ago changed Charlie forever, and now he is helping changes lives for God.

charlie hall

on

GOD LINKS

prayer

Here's what I've learned about prayer:

I am the prayer.
Your life is a living prayer. The way you live your life is incense to the Lord. You can't separate your life and your prayers.

Be natural.
Talk to God like you would to anyone else.

Ask for everything.
That includes things you think might "work themselves out." Invite God into every area and problem of your life.

Take "soul walks."
I often take walks during which I say to God, *I'm going to be with You and listen to You. God, this walk is about You and for You. I won't say anything or do anything without hearing from You. But I want You to speak to me about what I need to ask for.* When I do this, I find that an exchange goes on between my spirit and God's Spirit on a deeper level than when I just give God a list of prayer requests.

(Charlie is part of the Passion Tour. You can find him on the Web at www.generationproductions.com.)

The Next Step

When I graduated from high school, I left my home in Missouri and enrolled at Gordon College in Massachusetts with confidence that I *knew* God's plan for my life—to become a youth pastor. I studied hard, and the semesters seemed to fly by. Then, one summer between semesters, my dad challenged me to take a semester off from school and just spend that time with God seeking His direction for my life.

"But I already have God's direction," I argued.

"You *think* you know God's plan, but you need to be sure," Dad urged. "Read the Bible, and you'll see how many times problems arose because people didn't take the time to inquire of God and wait on Him for wisdom."

Still sure that I knew God's plan for my life, I took Dad's advice and moved home to Missouri. I lived at home and worked at Silver Dollar City for four months. During that time I spent a lot of time alone reading my Bible...and listening. And I realized that it wasn't just my dad urging me to take time to pray, but God Himself. At the end of those four months I knew only one thing for certain: God wanted me to add a second major to my studies and get a degree in political science.

Back at college, I added the political science classes to my curriculum and managed to graduate with a double major. After graduation, I worked as an intern with Senator John Ashcroft. As election time drew near, he asked me to work on his campaign, organizing voter registration. Ashcroft didn't win the election, but when President George

W. Bush appointed him as Attorney General, he invited me to go to Washington, D.C., with him, where I got the job of my dreams—working at the Department of Justice in the office of faith-based community initiatives.

As a teenager graduating from high school, I never could have imagined that God would take me to the Department of Justice in Washington, D.C., and that I would go on to manage campaigns and work for other political leaders. Thankfully, my father challenged me to take the time to seek God.

God didn't give me the whole road map for the rest of my life; He likely knew I couldn't handle it. But He gave me the next step.

At every crossroads of your life, take time to inquire of God.

He'll give you the next step. And God's next step may surprise you.

Jacob Herschend

will you Be Left Behind?

Marissa Morningstar kept her doubts to herself. She'd been raised in a Christian home, and everyone expected her to live a Christian life. She knew what her pastor and her parents believed about God. But Marissa honestly didn't know what *she* believed about God.

I'm just sixteen, Marissa reasoned. *It's too much to figure out who I am and how I'm supposed to fit into the high school crowd—much less figure out how I fit in the plans of the Creator of the universe!*

Occasionally she'd attend a youth conference and get on fire, but almost immediately doubts would plague her once again. *Does God exist? Is Jesus the Son of God? Is there a heaven and a hell? Is Jesus the only way to heaven? If He does exist, what does that have to do with me? And if He exists, does He even listen to my prayers after all the things I've done?*

Marissa didn't know what the big deal was about the movie *Left Behind,* but she settled into her seat as the theater went dark. The story began with a commercial airline pilot flying a transatlantic flight when the unimaginable occurs—hundreds of people simply disappear from the plane! Worse, people were disappearing all over the world. Airplanes, trains, and cars crashed when the people at the controls were beamed to some unseen place, leaving the whole world in chaos.

The event—the rapture of the church, when He will

take true believers to heaven in the twinkling of an eye—was prophesied in the Bible thousands of years before. The movie told the story of those who were left behind.

Marissa left the theater with one burning question: *What if I'm left behind?*

After the movie, Marissa's youth group discussed the seven very difficult years following the Rapture that the Bible calls the Tribulation. Marissa's stomach cramped into a hard knot, and she felt sick. Sobbing, she asked the kids in her youth group question after question.

"Is the Bible true?"

"How can we tell if we're saved?"

"What if we don't live up to God's standards?"

"How can we be sure Christianity is the right religion?"

No one could answer her. "Just read your Bible," they said. "Don't worry."

But Marissa *was* worried—very worried. If the Bible was true, Jesus could come at any time—and she would be left behind. That night she went to bed agonizing over her doubts and fears. "If You're real, I need to hear from You," she prayed. "Help me to believe! Help me to know You!"

Nothing.

Night after night, Marissa cried out to God for answers. Then, about a week later, she fell into a deep sleep and dreamed about Judgment Day. In the dream she sat at a table with three of her friends. Each of them was instructed to sign her name in a book and answer two questions by checking yes or no.

Do you believe in God?

Are you living for God?

Marissa checked yes. All three of her friends checked no.

A dark angel took her friends away, but a bright angel took Marissa to a huge, amazingly bright throne. God spoke to her and answered her questions. He told her that everything was going to be okay—she just had to pray and have faith.

Marissa awoke the next morning filled with peace. *It wasn't just a dream,* she thought. *God heard my prayers and answered my cry!*

Since then, Marissa prays with confidence for family and friends. She's determined to do her part to make sure none of them are left behind.

GOD LINKS

Psalm 62:8 tells us to pour out our hearts to God, for He is our refuge. We don't have to act like we've got it together or try to look good before God. After all, He sees and knows our hearts anyway. He wants us to take off our masks and be real in prayer. Pride keeps us from being completely honest and prompts us to resist acknowledging that we've had a wrong idea of God or, like Marissa, haven't known Him at all. Be totally honest with God…and He will be faithful to answer your cry!

Choosing God's Best

When I was five years old, my dad told me to ask God for wisdom. He explained to me what the Bible tells about King Solomon, the wisest man who ever lived. Solomon was king of Israel when God offered to give him anything he wanted. Solomon could have asked for riches, but he didn't. He could have asked for a long life, but he didn't. He could have asked for great fame, but he didn't. He even could have asked for the death of his enemies, but he didn't.

Solomon asked for wisdom.

The Bible says that God was so pleased with Solomon's request that He made him the wisest man in the world. He was so wise that kings and queens traveled from distant lands to meet him. If that wasn't enough—God also gave him great riches, long life, honor, fame, and peace from all his enemies.

Even at the age of five, that sounded good to me. I started regularly asking God for wisdom. Nothing fancy, just a heartfelt plea that God would make me wise like Solomon and help me tell right from wrong when I wasn't sure. The older I became, the more I learned that wisdom touches every part of life: friends, choices, romance, and career.

When I reached high school, like everyone else, I wanted a girl on my arm who would make me look better. But the wisdom I'd been praying for all those years began to show me that the choices I made about girls and how I treated them was based on the world's values—not God's. I realized that I was on a very slippery path that could lead me away from purity. I wanted to make the most of my single years and prepare to be a good husband for the wife God chose for me.

I realized that how a person chooses to date isn't a black-and-white issue, or necessarily a right-and-wrong one. That's what makes being a Christian both an adventure and a challenge: We don't always get a list of what we can and cannot do. We have choices. I decided that I didn't want to just do what God "allowed." I wanted to choose what wisdom is all about—God's best.

After prayerfully seeking God's wisdom for my life, I made a radical choice. I decided to kiss dating good-bye. Instead of dating, I chose to seek God. Instead of using women for what they could do for me, I chose to honor and respect them as daughters of God. Most radical of all, I decided to let wisdom direct *all* of my life—my choices, my career, and, yes, even my future wife.

I will never be the king of Israel or the wisest man in the world. But the most valuable lesson I ever learned was that of all the things you can get in this world the most important is wisdom.

A lot has changed in my life since I first started praying for wisdom, but my need for it has not. Today as a husband, father, and young pastor, I realize more than ever how much I need wisdom, and I'm asking God to give me wisdom beyond my years.

Joshua Harris

GOD LINKS

Here are some Scriptures to help you pray for wisdom:

1 Kings 3:4-14
You can read Solomon's story here.

Proverbs 15:33
Wisdom starts with fearing God.

Proverbs 16:16
Wisdom is better than wealth.

Ephesians 1:17
We need wisdom to know Christ better.

James 1:5
Here's an invitation to pray for wisdom.

James 3:17
This is what wisdom looks like.

(To order Joshua's bestselling books, *I Kissed Dating Goodbye* and *Boy Meets Girl*, or for more information, visit www.joshharris.com.)

5 if YOU'RE PRAYING ALONE...

Prayer is the most important work in the kingdom of God.

O. Hallesby

Together for Eternity

I was three years old when my whole world fell apart. I didn't understand what *divorce* meant. I couldn't help but wonder if it meant that I was a very bad girl. No matter how I cried and begged, I couldn't live with my mother and daddy anymore. I couldn't even live in my house.

My parents sent me to live with my grandmother. She took me to church and taught me all about Jesus. I learned that He loved me and wouldn't leave me. Every week at prayer service, I got down on my knees at the altar and prayed for God to rescue my family. And in my bedroom at night, I cried out to God to save my parents.

When I was twelve, my life got turned upside down again. I was sent to live with my mother and stepfather. They didn't go to church and never made arrangements for me to go. And deep inside me a ball of pain and anger started to grow. I discovered that, at least briefly, alcohol numbed the pain in my heart. I began to party and hide things from my parents. My relationship with God wasn't important to me anymore. I didn't even care if my parents got saved.

After a few years, God put people in my life who helped me see what I'd given up. I turned back to God, and He melted the hurt and pain I'd carried around since I was three. When I was fifteen, I told my mom that I wanted to go to church and that I wanted my family to go with me. Once again I began praying earnestly for my parents' salvation.

At first, Mom just dropped me off at church and sped away. But after a while, she and my younger sister started going in with me. Being in church softened my mom's heart, and she cried through every song and the entire sermon. It wasn't long before my mom and sister gave their hearts and lives to Jesus.

We all continued to pray for my stepfather, but he didn't make it easy. He didn't go to church, but spent his Sundays on the golf course. But you know what God did? He met my stepfather right where he was—on the golf course!

One Sunday he was golfing alone when he met another man who was on his own. The two men joined forces and got to know one another while they golfed. The other man was a Christian, and right there on the golf course he told my stepfather about Jesus, and my stepfather became a Christian!

I can't change the fact that my family broke apart when

I was three. And I can't go back and relive those years with my family. What I can do is thank God for my grandmother and make sure, through prayer, that my family will never be separated in eternity—and remember that all things are possible with Him!

Kimberly Houston

A price to Be Paid

I was raised in a large Muslim family with dozens of aunts, uncles, and cousins who were integral parts of my life. My sister, Jean, and I were especially close. We attended a high school with thirty-five different nationalities represented. Eighty-five percent of our student body was Muslim. That's why I was furious with Jean that September morning as we got ready for school. She was going to pray at the flagpole that morning.

My own sister had gone off the deep end.

She'd done something that was inexcusable in our family.

She had converted to Christianity.

Of course, the entire family reacted with hostility. Why wouldn't we, when Jean had turned her back on our faith? Instead of being best friends, now we barely spoke to one another. When Jean attempted to talk to me about Jesus, I refused to listen. And I refused her invitations to church.

Doesn't she get it? Being a Christian isn't acceptable.

I was furious to see her standing alone at the flagpole, praying.

I knew that Islam was the true religion, but I couldn't deny the change I saw in Jean as the months passed. Her whole demeanor changed. Before, she'd been chronically angry and semidepressed; now she glowed with hope and joy.

What's gotten into her? I wondered as I watched her blossom into a happy person. When Jean invited me to her church's all-night New Year's Eve party, I agreed to go for the dinner and fun. I had no idea there would also be worship, a message, and prayer. But the Christians didn't win me over.

Two days later, I told Jean I would go to church with her again. "But don't get excited," I warned her. "You're wrong about your religion. Being a Muslim is right."

The truth is that I was drawn to the love and joy I could see in the youth at Jean's church. After the morning service the youth pastor sat with me and answered my questions. Confronted by God's great love, I couldn't resist it. Knowing full well the hostility I would face, I gave my life to Jesus.

I would like to say that our family embraced us and accepted our right to worship as we chose. That would make a great story, but it didn't happen. Twelve aunts and uncles, sixty first cousins, and numerous second cousins met with our family to decide the fate of "the girls who converted," as we were known.

They voted to disown us.

At school, our lockers were arranged alphabetically, which meant my locker was surrounded by my cousins' lockers. We were used to talking and joking each morning before school. But since we were no longer family, our cousins couldn't associate with us. That was a bad way to start each morning, but even worse, in each of my six classes the students peppered me with hostile questions.

"How could God have a son?"

"Who is Jesus?"

"How could you possibly believe that Jesus died on a cross?"

"Why have you turned away from your faith?"

I didn't have answers for them, but every day God calmed my heart, and I steadied my resolve to follow Jesus. Jean and I started a Bible study on campus, and three other students joined us.

We lost our large, loving family, but God replaced them with church members who invited us to Sunday dinners and holiday gatherings and stood in the place of our biological family for us.

When the next year rolled around, Jean had graduated and gone to college. I stood at the flagpole, but I wasn't alone. A Christian teacher and a Romanian student stood alongside me, praying that God's Spirit would impact the school and change lives.

Since then, I have graduated from high school, and both of "the girls who converted" are still following Jesus. We both finished college, and Jean works for the Red Cross, where she plans to work with people subjected to political injustices.

I now work on a church staff and am involved in planting a church for Arabs and Muslims in my area. I also desire to become a missionary to the Middle East.

Jean and I have paid a high price to become Christians. But Jesus is worth it all.

Catherine Chammout

GOD LINKS

see you at the pole

Forty-five thousand teens showed up at their flagpoles for the first See You at the Pole event on the third Wednesday of September 1991. In the years since that first meeting, thousands of student-led Bible clubs and prayer groups have formed as a result of SYATP, and millions of teens have gathered on that day to pray for their schools. Whether you are the only student praying at the flagpole as Catherine's sister Jean was, or one of a thousand strong, know that God will use your prayers as you stand for Him and intercede for your school.

You can log on to www.syatp.com to tell your school's SYATP story or read suggestions and inspiring testimonies. For more information on how you can help rally students in your area to pray, call

858-451-1111
or go to
www.youthworkers.net.

Through the Eyes of Jesus

When I stepped into the hallway of my high school, I was shaking. There were tons of students all around, but I felt all alone. I peered into the faces of people I knew as they passed me, trying to envision what they'd think of me. Then I looked down the hall and saw the crowds of people around my locker, and my heart felt as if it was going to burst out of my chest. *Did I really want to do this?*

I'd heard a message recently on living a life of no reputation. While I was listening, it suddenly occurred to me that in my four years of high school I'd won lots of recognition for my reputation—but it was all wrapped up in my reputation as a jock.

Sitting there, a wave of sadness swept over me when I realized that although many people knew my name, most of them didn't know the God I serve. In those moments I felt Him leading me to kneel down in front of my locker, to lay down my reputation, and to open myself for persecution as I prayed for my campus.

I wanted to follow God's leading, but I knew nobody would join me. In fact, they'd make fun of me.

I whispered to a friend walking beside me, "I can't do this." Then I muttered a prayer, silently asking the Lord for boldness and courage to follow through. When I looked up again, it was as if my vision was wiped clean and I saw my classmates through different eyes—the eyes of Jesus. I no longer saw the surface stuff; their smiles had disappeared. Instead I saw the pain, guilt, and confusion underneath. My

heart ached as the Spirit convicted me of my own selfish-
ness.

Then I knelt by my locker and thanked God. I asked
Him to touch my campus and to use me any way He wanted
in the remaining weeks of school. I don't know what God
did in my classmates as a result of my prayers, but He did a
lot in me. As radical and scary as getting out of my comfort
zone was, I'm already experiencing the rewards as I grow by
leaps and bounds in my walk with Jesus.

From now on, if my friends look for me, they'd better
look low, because between class periods every school day
until graduation I'll be found kneeling and praying in obedience to God's calling.

Christina Bock

6 IF THINGS TURN VIOLENT...

When the enemy shall come in like a flood,
the Spirit of the LORD shall lift up
a standard against him.

Isaiah 59:19b, KJV

safety in september

September—that month that betrays summer—has never been my favorite month. In spite of the onset of fall, it was a beautiful Wednesday morning when I arrived at school early for marching-band practice. Band practice was a great excuse to miss praying at the flagpole that one day of the year. But I couldn't get out of the youth rally held at Wedgwood Baptist Church that evening because I was part of the youth drama.

I had to be at the church by 5 P.M. to rehearse our skit. Nothing seemed unusual, and we had a good time blocking our scenes and practicing our lines. The tech crew was there and the band showed up. People began trickling into the sanctuary early—kids were coming from all over town for the rally.

I posted myself near an outside door to pass out programs and watch for a friend who was coming. I nodded to groups that entered and greeted as many as possible. Then I saw a tall man walk inside—I had a strange feeling that something wasn't right. I turned to watch him walk into the lobby, and chills rippled up my spine.

He had a gun in his jeans!

Before I could react, the man started firing at people in the hallway.

He's killing people in the church building! I've got to help them!

It never occurred to me to run away from the building—I ran inside.

If he can't see me, he can't kill me, I thought, trying to calm the terror that shook me. I had just knelt behind a pew in the back row when I heard a series of rapid shots and felt searing pain explode in my back with such intensity that I had to gasp for air.

I've been shot!

Gripped by pain and fear, I did the only thing I *could* do: I prayed. I prayed harder and more fervently than I'd ever prayed in my life. *God help us! Protect us!*

More shots were fired in rapid succession, and I braced myself for another bullet.

Finally, the man turned the gun on himself.

The power of God helped me stand on my feet and walk outside to an ambulance.

I was whisked away to the hospital for treatment, but after the shooting, even the hospital didn't feel safer than the church—or any other place for that matter. The way I figured it, there is only one safe place on earth.

And that's in the center of God's perfect will, which is right where I want to be.

Mary Beth Talley

Eternity in Their Hearts

I had an urge to pray that fall, a few days before the See You at the Pole prayer rally at my high school. This urge to pray was unusual for me. Although I'd been a Christian for years and went to church regularly, like most teens I knew, I was pretty complacent. I certainly wasn't on fire for God and didn't do anything to help anyone else know Him.

In other words, I was pretty normal.

I showed up at the flagpole to pray along with a hundred other teens that morning. I had no idea it would be the last normal day of my life.

That evening I went to a youth rally at my church, Wedgwood Baptist in Fort Worth, Texas. I found a seat near my friends about four rows from the front. We were laughing, talking, and listening to the band when an explosion rocked the room.

That's gunfire! I thought.

Almost in slow motion, I turned to see glass shattering in the sanctuary.

I dived for cover as band members fell to the floor. I saw a gunman standing with his arm outstretched, firing rapidly at the people who stood next to the wall. Amid screams and the sounds of shots being fired, time no longer existed.

Scenes of carnage were flashing around me in freeze-frames, and I saw eternity. And with the clarity of vision that comes with the smell and sound of death, I knew that though eternity was ready for me…I was not ready for eternity.

The revelation was sudden and sharp and clear: My relationship with God was little more than fire insurance. And in the fires of eternity, it would burn. I had made a commitment to Jesus with my *head,* but never had I committed my life to Him with my *heart.*

In the room around me people were wounded and dying. For some of my friends, it was too late for last-minute revelations. On my knees, I prayed not from my head, but from the depth of my heart: *God, I don't have any control over this situation, but I have control over my destiny. I accept Jesus as my Savior, and I give my life to You. If I die tonight, I want to die for You. If I live, I want to live for You.*

I wanted this nightmare to be over, but the gunman just kept firing.

Then finally…*silence.*

The screaming of police car sirens, the moans of the wounded, and the mournful wailing for the dead overpowered my senses. I stumbled outside along with six hundred other people. Still moving in slow motion, I helped kids find their parents. I saw our youth pastor collapse in grief from seeing those who had been slaughtered. I was numb with shock, but at that moment I knew the truth of Romans 8:26: God helps us pray when we don't know how. I didn't know how to pray for our youth pastor who was suffering such loss, but God helped me. Afterward, he pulled himself up off the grass and went to minister to his flock.

I haven't lived a normal day since then—nor do I want to. I have glimpsed eternity, and I am now ready. Are you?

Kevin Pratt

GOD LINKS

Kevin committed his life to Christ in the midst of a tragedy. But you don't have to be involved in a disaster to realize that you need God—because God Himself is seeking after you! He knocks on the door of your heart, waiting for you to open up.

The Bible tells you how you can invite Jesus into your life and surrender to Him:

> If you confess with your mouth, "Jesus is Lord," and believe in your heart that God raised him from the dead, you will be saved.
>
> **Romans 10:9**

You don't have to say certain words; it's yielding your heart that matters. But this prayer could be a springboard to get you started: *Lord, I'm aware that I'm not right with You. Please forgive me for my sins. Come into my life and make Yourself real to me. I know I need You! I give my life to You and thank You for dying on the cross for me.*

7

IF YOU WANT GOD TO MOVE AT YOUR SCHOOL...

A "prayer warrior" is a person who is convinced that God is omnipotent—that God has the power to do anything, to change anyone, and to intervene in any circumstance.

Bill Hybels

Canada fire

God didn't fit in any of the cliques at South Delta Secondary School in Canada. The stereotypes of Christians were deep-seated and narrowly defined. At one time, a group of Christians had met in an empty classroom to talk, watch videos, play games, and eat pizza. They spent the lunch hour inside their "club room," ignoring the people who ate alone in the hallways. Not much more than a special club for the elite, the group shrank in size and never reached out to help the troubled teens around them.

A Bible study also met in the same room. Their format included discussing Bible passages and arguing over what each verse meant. Since most of the meetings ended with students squabbling over who was right and who was wrong, that group attracted only teens who liked to argue.

Another Christian activity at South Delta was See You at the Pole. On the third Wednesday of September, a group of students, led by a few youth pastors, met and prayed for the school. But afterward, everyone dispersed to their cliques and groups of friends.

So those were the stereotypes that defined the word *Christian* at Darian Kovak's high school: either a person so much better than everyone else that he needed a special club, someone who liked to argue, or someone who met only once a year for a few minutes of public prayer.

That's why when Darian heard an American student named Matt challenge Canadian teens to start prayer groups at their high schools, he knew that it would be difficult— God already had a pretty bad rap at South Delta. The idea of teens breaking through those stereotypes and crossing the boundaries of cliques seemed remote. Still, Darian signed a sheet requesting more information. Soon he received e-mails from Matt with suggestions about how to start a prayer group.

Darian knew it would take more than good intentions for teens to gather for prayer at his high school. It would take a miracle.

Then one night at his youth group, a girl named Jess asked Darian if he'd ever thought about praying at school. *There it is again,* Darian thought, amazed that he would be getting these promptings from two different people. Spurred on by Jess's encouragement, the next day during lunch, Darian and Jess gathered some students around the flagpole to pray.

The next week they met again, and a few others joined them. The following week even more teens showed up. Each week, Darian opened with a short devotion and read a psalm. Then the students broke into groups of three to pray specifically for teachers or individual students they knew. One group prayed for the football team.

From the beginning the group determined to be all-inclusive, inviting everyone to join. One of their specific prayers was that God would pull down the barriers that divided students and bring unity.

When an unsaved student stopped by to check out what they were doing, he was welcomed and encouraged. Another student came and asked for prayer for his sick father. One by one, people with real needs arrived asking for prayer—each at different levels spiritually and socially. Somehow, each person felt accepted.

One rainy, wintry day a teacher opened the student council room and ushered the shivering students inside. They relished the warmth, the comfortable chairs, and the opportunity to use a piano. When a student brought his guitar, they added worship to their prayer time.

"It blew me away," Darian recalls. "I never thought something like this would happen in my school."

Week after week, the group grew. At the beginning of the following school year nearly seventy students, along with an occasional teacher or two, showed up each week to pray. And amazingly, people from all the various student groups felt welcome. And as the focus remained on praying for the school, the stereotypes of Christians began to fall away. Walls crumbled, barriers collapsed…and deep friendships emerged. And for the first time the gospel was shared openly with unsaved students.

Darian graduated at the end of the second year of the prayer group, and other students took up the challenge of continuing what he had begun. As Darian prepared for college, his heart lingered in prayer over his high school and other schools across Canada. Day after day, he prayed that the fire of God would sweep Canada.

So while he was in college, Darian started Canada Fire, a ministry dedicated to spreading the vision for prayer groups in schools all across the country. Darian met the president of Focus on the Family Canada, who spread the word through a letter to subscribers. A man from his church purchased, designed, and now maintains a web site, www.canadafire.org, to further spread the vision. Soon, Darian was asked to speak at youth groups, churches, and conferences.

All across the nation, teens are lifting the torch of prayer to God. Lives are being changed, schools are experiencing the presence of the Holy Spirit, and Canada is alight with the fire of God.

GOD LINKS

3 steps to reach your campus

To connect with Canada Fire, visit www.canadafire.org. And to seek God for your high school:

1.

Get in God's presence.

2.

Listen to His voice.

3.

Do what He says.

Dream big and don't be afraid to ask for big things!

Death Threats at Sapulpa High

Just a few weeks after the shootings at Columbine in Littleton, Colorado, a copycat made death threats at Sapulpa High School near Tulsa, Oklahoma. A note was found in the restroom that named students who were targeted to die. The administrators added extra security and attempted to control panic among the student body. As one of the leaders of the Christian club at school, I felt that the situation needed a more drastic approach: Students needed to know that God was real and that He could change the hardest of hearts.

When Ricky, a former drug dealer whose life had been radically changed by the power of God, heard about the death threats, he was ready to act. He decided to stand up in the cafeteria, give his testimony, and lead others in prayer.

This is it, God! I prayed. *This is the opportunity we've been waiting for!*

Ricky and I gathered a dozen of our Christian friends and canceled our lunchtime club meeting. Instead, we went to the gym and humbled ourselves before God, crying out for Him to touch our school.

Then we headed to the cafeteria. When Ricky began telling what God had done for him, he was sent to the principal's office. But one by one, other students stood up in Ricky's place and shared the plan of salvation. A Russian foreign-exchange student who could barely speak English stood up to testify.

Teachers, administrators, and the school superintendent came to the cafeteria, but the students wouldn't stop. It was clear that if they took one teen to the principal's office, another would take his place. Instead of interfering, the staff watched from the sidelines.

When the Holy Spirit nudged me to speak, I urged everyone to let go of anything—drugs, alcohol, or relationships—that kept them from Jesus. Some students wept openly, some asked questions, and five committed their lives to Jesus.

Not only were the death threats not carried out at Sapulpa High School, but the power of fear was broken, and God gave Christians a new boldness. A few weeks later one of my friends who had once been on drugs performed a drama and gave her testimony in front of nine hundred people at a junior high talent show. Two hundred people filed to the front of the auditorium and gave their lives to Jesus.

God turned our fear into faith in Him. Students who had been complacent now had the courage to stand for Christ—not only in the lunchroom, but also in the halls, on the football field, and wherever they went.

Julee DeLong

GOD LINKS

7 prayer principles for your campus

1.
Remember that your campus prayer ministry will only be as effective as your personal prayer time.

2.
Be led by the Holy Spirit. Invite Him to move freely.

3.
Ask God for His prayer strategy for your campus.

4.
Ask your administrators and teachers how you can pray specifically for them.

5.
Pray for the salvation of specific students on your campus and for chances to share Christ with them.

6.
Pray for everyone on your campus.

7.
Be specific in your prayers. Write them down, and then watch and wait for the answers.

(Adapted from Terry Johnson's *A Guide to Starting a Prayer Group on Your Campus*, as it appeared in *Frontlines*, a newsletter of Campus Ministry Network, Andover, Kansas.)

The Most Holy place

My high school was a tough place in 1999. Fights broke out in the hall and kids threatened to shoot other kids. Kids got beat up, and a feeling of chaos seemed to blanket the school—kids running up and down the halls screaming. The school board installed metal detectors to check for weapons, but that didn't solve the problem. I knew that things needed to change and that it would take a miracle from God for that to happen. Knowing that put me in a tough spot. I realized that God was the answer, but I wasn't comfortable talking to others about Him.

To be honest, there was another problem. I'd been an outcast for a long time, and the last thing I wanted was to be even more of an outcast in high school because of speaking out. I was torn between what would be best for the school and what might be best for me. But was keeping my mouth shut and trying to protect my reputation best for *anyone?*

The summer before the new school year, I read in the Bible about how the curtain in the temple that separated the Holy Place from the Most Holy Place ripped in two when Jesus died. At that moment all of us—not just the high priest—were given access to the Most Holy Place. For some reason, realizing that through prayer I had direct access to God made me want to pray. I decided to pray and do whatever God directed me to do.

The day before school started, I met with some of my friends, and we did a Jericho Walk around the perimeter of the high school. We walked it six times, praying for specific students, teachers, and administrators. We prayed about addictions some kids were struggling with, and we prayed peace over the whole school. On the last lap we sang songs and praised God. That night I had a strong sense that things would change.

Once school started, I met with several friends every morning at 7:00 to pray. One of the boys I prayed for was Chris, a high school dropout who was on drugs. As weeks passed, the prayer group grew to forty kids. Before, none of us knew the other Christians at our school, but now many of us carried Bibles. We got to know one another and grew bold in our faith.

I began a Bible study in the basement of my home, and about fifteen kids attended. And one night, who showed up for Bible study but Chris! That night he gave his life to Jesus. Not long afterward, I felt an urge to talk to a girl in my second-hour class. She didn't believe in Jesus and was involved in Wicca, a type of witchcraft.

She told me that church was too complicated. "Jesus isn't complicated!" I said. "He's all about grace!" Then I explained about the temple curtain being torn and how, by His sacrifice on the cross, Jesus provided salvation for every-one—including her—and direct access to God.

I can't say that God swept through the entire school or that all the problems disappeared. That didn't happen. But God swept through lives—one by one. The school year wasn't perfect, but it was the most peaceful year anyone could remember.

I thank God every day that there's no limit to the Most Holy Place—that no matter your age or need, God invites you to His throne of grace.

Anyone is welcome…anytime.

Tyler Branine

GOD LINKS

God tells us that there is a power in agreement and that where two or three of us are gathered in the name of Jesus, He is there in our midst (see Matthew 18:19–20). And breaking into small groups makes it easier for most teens to pray. That's why small-group prayer is so effective.

You could meet at the flagpole every morning before school to pray, pray at lunch with your group, or have an evening prayer gathering. (Even though it's legal for students to gather in a public school to pray, it's best to ask for permission from your school administration.)

Here are some ideas for small-group praying:

— Tyler's prayer group gathered at his yellow truck in the school parking lot and prayed every morning. They prayed specifically for students in three ways: by name, by what they struggled with, and about their relationship with God. When students asked them what they were doing out by Tyler's truck, the pray-ers had a great opportunity to tell them about Christ.

— Some groups start with praise.

— One group focuses on a specific prayer target each day. One day they might pray for teachers; on another, for salvation or revival. Others take daily prayer requests.

— Another group asked for prayer support from local churches, and adults in that community are now praying for the campus prayer warriors.

Triple the Power

It was easy to identify what was wrong at my high school—division, drugs, drinking, and sex dominated many of the students' lives. But it wasn't so easy to identify a solution. In the summer of 2001, I attended a Student Venture convention in Myrtle Beach, South Carolina, and roomed with Rachel Gartrell and Cortney Moore, who were also students at McEachern High School.

We agreed that what we most wanted was to see unity between the Christian students at our high school develop so that we might be more bold as witnesses. Everything seemed to work against unity because our school was large and spread out in multiple buildings across a large campus. Still, we prayed together at the beach, and formed a "prayer triplet" to continue praying throughout the summer, asking for God's strategies.

Little by little, God gave us His plan. Before school started, we joined a few other Christian students on a prayer walk around the campus, asking God to tear down the walls of division.

Our next idea was awesome! We threw a "Beauty-Bash Sleepover" for freshman, sophomore, and junior girls. Besides doing their hair and nails, we provided food and all-night fun. Before the party ended, the seniors washed the underclassmen's feet to show that we wanted to serve them and establish relationships with them.

God's next strategy was a Bible study for cheerleaders. Cortney and I, both varsity cheerleaders, started a Bible study to reach out to friends. Although it started small, within a few weeks many more cheerleaders joined the group.

Next, for Senior Week, we planned a senior girls breakfast and invited Nancy Wilson of Student Venture to speak. We thought maybe 50 seniors would come, but *150* showed up! They all heard the gospel, and nine accepted Jesus as Lord and Savior.

God inspired Rachel to design a red T-shirt for all the senior girls to wear on the same day, which created unity among them and brought girls from different ethnic groups and religions together and increased their openness to God.

Then, after the terrorist attacks on September 11, students were allowed to leave their classes to pray. Out of three thousand students, three hundred joined together for one purpose: to pray for our nation; for the president; for our leaders; for firefighters, police, and rescue workers; and for all those who lost loved ones in the tragedy.

At a schoolwide assembly, the principle called our senior class "the class of unity." It was wonderful to graduate with his stamp of approval, but it was even more awesome to know that we would leave McEachern High with God's approval.

Katie McElreath

GOD LINKS

PRAYER TRIPLETS

The Prayer Triplet strategy is the simplest, most widespread movement of ongoing prayer among teens today. It's a great way to mobilize friends to pray! Here are some of the ways you can use it:

- Your triplet could be from your sports team, school club, or youth group.

- Many triplet efforts involve three Christian friends meeting three times a week to pray for three friends who need Jesus. That means *nine friends* are being prayed for!

- As Katie, Cortney, and Rachel did, you could regularly pray for each other and your school and do an outreach together to show God's love.

- Your triplet could pray for those whose locker is next to each of you or pray one page a week through the pages of your high school yearbook.

- If you don't have a group to pray with, ask God to bring two others to form a triplet with you. Then trust Him to provide!

For more information, visit www.gocampus.org or www.everyschool.com.

8 iF YOU'RE ABOUT TO GIVE UP...

Our prayers lay the track down on which
God's power can come.

Watchman Nee

Drug of choice

I was seventeen years old, and although I had rededicated
my life to Jesus and was trying to follow God, my Christian
walk was on a gradual downhill slide. To make matters
worse, the youth group I attended wasn't going well for me.
I spent hours at the church working on electronics, light,
and sound for the teen center, and all I got in return was a
bad case of burnout. Part of me wanted to ditch the whole
thing and go back to hanging out with my old friends and
doing drugs.

But what's going to happen if I turn my back on God again? I
worried. *What will happen to the younger teens that look up to me?*

The worship team always talked about getting together to pray, but it never happened. Our frustrations mounted because the adults didn't trust us to lead worship the way they thought best, so they shot down all our visions and ideas.

I was not experiencing the joy of the Lord. *If this is what being a Christian is all about,* I thought, *I'll just drop out of the worship band and the church!*

To complicate matters even further, I met a girl. Wow. I loved hanging out with her...even though she practiced witchcraft and voodoo and used drugs. I was free-falling headfirst back into my old lifestyle.

Then one night, Derek, the drummer for the worship team, asked me to join him and another guitar player at his house to pray and talk about things. I was on my way to the girl's house to do drugs that night, but I thought, *One quick prayer, then I'm outta there.*

Some worship music began playing, and the three of us got down on our knees to pray. When I prayed, "God, we need help," I meant, "God, *I* really need help!"

Then we began praying for more of God. Suddenly, the presence of God came upon us so heavily that we fell on our faces, sobbing and broken before the Lord. I was mortified that God even showed up to talk to me when I was so full of sin.

Our prayers became so fervent that Derek's parents were afraid the neighbors would call the police. But we heard the voice of the Lord say, *What I've started, no man or woman can stop. You are a holy army, and I'm equipping you. My banner over you is love.*

What began as a five-minute prayer turned into a five-hour prayer vigil. Needless to say, I didn't go over to that girl's house that night. In fact, the only time I saw her after that was when I took her to my youth group. And I haven't used drugs again.

After experiencing the presence of God, well, drugs aren't even in the same league as a high like that.

Stosh Coale

GOD LINKS

Breaking through to god

How can you keep your prayers full of life? If your prayers seem dull and your soul feels dry like Stosh's did, ask yourself these questions. They'll help you keep your prayer times fresh:

- What sin in my life is keeping me from breaking through?

- What area of my life am I not letting God deal with?

- Am I preventing Jesus from being Lord of something in my life?

- What is keeping me from having the closest possible relationship with God?

Now just sit and listen for a few minutes. God will open your eyes and begin to speak to you. When you ask, *Lord, what needs to be purified?* He may show you your jealousy, pride, or the way you treat people. It may be your attitude. Ask Him to cleanse your heart. You can have a fresh encounter with God every day if you come to Him with this attitude:

Create in me a clean heart, O God.

Psalm 51:10, NLT

first priority

God, I know You want First Priority on our campus, Becky prayed. *But I keep running into brick walls! I'm so frustrated that I want to quit! Help me to persevere through this hard time and to be strong! Lord, bring everything into order. Help me find dedicated leaders and students who'll stand up for You.* Becky found herself praying this prayer almost nightly.

She had first heard about First Priority—an on-campus ministry—at the end of her sophomore year of high school. It wasn't just a Christian club or Bible study for believers. This was an outreach with a focus on unsaved students, and she knew it was just what her high school needed. So many students were hurting and without hope. Many were into drugs and alcohol or sex or were struggling with eating disorders and abusive situations. Scores of unchurched teens attended her public high school in Monroe, Washington— and she wanted all of them to know Jesus.

More than anything, Becky wanted to start a First Priority outreach at her high school. But how could she get other Christians on her campus to catch the vision? They only seemed interested in their own lives and hanging out with friends.

Despite these obstacles, during her junior year, Becky put all her efforts into starting the club. But no matter what she tried, she couldn't get First Priority going. She couldn't find Christian students who would be dedicated and stand up for their faith. Most were more interested in their popularity or were scared about what people would think if they reached out to other students. She couldn't find leaders or get anything approved by the administration. So she kept praying…and praying…and praying.

And the more Becky prayed, the more she realized that *prayer was the answer.* It wasn't a last resort. All her efforts were nothing without prayer. It was the first thing—the best thing—she could do to pave the way for God to work on her campus.

But there were plenty of times when she felt she could hardly go on, when everything looked impossible. *Where are You, God? I thought You wanted this on our campus! I need Your help! Bring everything into order and bring leaders who are determined and committed.* Becky cried out to the Lord on discouraging days when, after another defeat, she came home in tears.

Only one friend from church, Justin, would occasionally pray with her. But Becky wouldn't give up—she kept praying and doing what she could to start the club throughout her junior year and the next summer, but without any success. Becky could see that students were hungry for something, and she *knew* that God was the answer. And something or Someone kept urging her on.

Finally, at the beginning of her senior year, Becky invited the one hundred students who'd showed up at the See You at the Pole gathering to the first meeting of First Priority. When fifty teens signed up, Becky was elated. But the obstacles didn't end there: She would call twenty people who had signed their names to join, and only three or four would show up for leadership meetings. And at the next meeting, a different three would show up. There were many disappointments and setbacks, and the details for First Priority didn't come together right away—and Becky couldn't stop praying.

But by the middle of the year, Becky had a strong leadership core of students who were passionate about the campus, some teachers who were cheering them on, and over one hundred students who were showing up for their weekly lunchtime First Priority meetings. By the spring, twenty-six students had committed their lives to Christ and had their lives totally changed, and when Becky left for college, she passed leadership on to a very determined and passionate group of students who wanted to reach every student on their campus for God.

Because prayer had become her *first resource,* many students at her high school made Jesus their *first priority* that year and in the years since.

GOD LINKS

first priority

A unique outreach ministry for high school campuses, First Priority has a series of weekly lunch gatherings including:

Accountability Week
Students get in small groups and share what God is doing in their lives and support each other spiritually.

Challenge Week
A guest speaker is brought in to challenge the students.

Testimony and Prayer Week
Students give their testimonies about what God has done in their lives.

Seek Week
The gospel is presented and an altar call given.

For more information, visit
www.firstpriority.org
or
www.reachthecampus.com

sending out an sos

I was a teen on fire for Jesus. You know the type. I helped others settle their doubts about Christianity. I also led a youth group at church and was involved with evangelism at school. But I had no idea how drastically my faith would be tested when, at the age of sixteen, I moved to the port city of Mersin, Turkey, as a foreign-exchange student.

I lived with a Turkish family, attended a Turkish school, and met new Turkish friends every day. After a few months, I knew how to speak Turkish well enough to teach English at my high school. A few teachers befriended me, and the English teachers' lounge became my favorite hangout. In Mersin I met Muslims who were as passionate about Islam as I was about Christianity. They were as concerned about my eternal destiny as I was about theirs.

But spending months in a Muslim nation without a place to worship had taken its toll. I felt a desperate need for Christian fellowship. I had met one Christian missionary, Carolyn, but I'd only seen her twice in all the months I'd been in Turkey. I never realized until then how much I took my church and Christian friends for granted. I felt like my spiritual zeal was drying up.

Gradually, questions about God, Jesus, and the Bible crept into my mind. I began to wonder if God was even real. And those doubts about fundamental issues terrified me. Out of desperation one night, I prayed, *God, knock me off my feet if You have to, but make me know that You are real! And send Christians to me!*

God didn't speak in an audible voice or write on the wall, so I went to school the next day hanging on to my faith—by faith. I overheard people talking about a ship that had just arrived in Mersin. From their conversation, I gathered that it was some kind of international floating library that sold English books. The faculty agreed that it would make an ideal field trip for the English classes, so they arranged for vans and enlisted me to go as a translator.

When we arrived at the ship, we learned that the crew was made up of more than three hundred people from more than thirty countries. The Turkish students toured the entire vessel, seeing where the crew slept and ate, where the engineers worked, and where the captain steered the ship. After the tour the students were allowed to browse and shop for books.

I noticed a man walk by carrying a leather-bound book. The cloth bookmark and silver-trimmed pages tipped me off that it must be a Bible. I recalled the desperation of my prayer the night before. *Has God sent me a Christian?*

I approached the man. "Are you a Christian?"

"Yes, I am!" he replied with a huge smile.

"By chance is there a church service on the ship?"

"There is, and if you'd like to attend, I'll ask my supervisor if you can come."

God's faithfulness in answering my prayer left me awestruck. After school, I went back to the ship hoping to find the Christian I'd met. Instead, I saw Carolyn.

"Don't you know what this ship is?" she asked. "It's the

Doulos, and it belongs to Operation Mobilization. The crew members are all Christians, and they stopped in Mersin to minister for a week."

Carolyn and I talked in Turkish, which alerted the man sitting across the table that I could translate. He asked me to help translate for the crew while they were docked in Mersin. I felt like a starving man who'd just been invited to a feast.

I spent the next several days on the ship, talking and praying with the crew, translating, and attending church services and prayer meetings. It was like being plunged into a rushing river after being in the middle of a scorched desert! I had prayed for a few Christians, and God sent me three hundred!

A few days later, I learned that the *Doulos* hadn't intended to dock at Mersin at all. Its next destination had been Cyprus, but at the last minute the government of Cyprus canceled its invitation. The ship suddenly found itself in the middle of the Mediterranean with nowhere to go. After studying charts and maps, the captain set course for Mersin.

Here's how it seems to have happened: I was in Mersin crying out for God to send Christians. In response, God stopped a ship in the middle of the Mediterranean with a three-hundred-member Christian crew, made them change course, and sent them to me.

Okay, that knocked me off my feet. God really hears and answers our prayers. His answer to me erased my doubts and reignited my passion for Him.

Ryan Keating

9

if YOU'RE ON THE WRONG PATH...

The revival that God promises begins when we humble ourselves, repent, fast, pray, and seek His face and turn from our evil ways. God has promised to respond with revival fire for any person who will hear, love, trust, and obey Him.

Bill Bright

Shackled by sin

For five years, I had been struggling with an addiction to pornography—a battle I was losing. I had become a Christian two years before, but my addiction took even my love of God hostage. It's not that I didn't pray. I did—usually while looking at porn sites on the Internet. Lust consumed me, and I felt powerless to change.

One Sunday morning I sat in the sanctuary half-listening to the sermon. My thoughts were on a verse from Psalm 121: "I lift up my eyes to the hills—where does my help come from? My help comes from the LORD, the Maker of heaven and earth."

I wanted to believe that God could rescue me, but there I was, sitting in church yet living a double life. *People at church think I'm a strong teen role model,* I thought. *My family thinks I'm a devoted Christian. The truth is that I'm neither. I lift up my eyes to the hills, but help comes from nowhere.*

Seconds later, my attention was riveted to the words spoken from the pulpit. "The LORD detests men of perverse heart but he delights in those whose ways are blameless" (Proverbs 11:20).

God detests me? The thought shocked and horrified me. But why wouldn't He? I was a hypocrite and a liar. I was a failure in my faith. My ways were far from blameless. For the first time I saw my sin the way God saw it. I bowed my head and sent an urgent prayer to heaven. *God, if You are listening to me, hear my plea. I am a sinner and a slave to my sin. God, save me! I believe that You can, yet I'm still shackled. Relieve me of this burden—please. I have no other options.*

I hurried out of the church, avoiding everyone I knew from my youth group. At home, I fell on my bed and stared into space for half an hour until my mom knocked on the door.

"Honey," she said, "I just got a call from the church. One of the kids can't go to camp, and the camp fee is nonrefundable. They want to know if you'll go in his place. Interested?"

I need to get away from that computer and think about something else.

"Yeah, I'll go…"

"Are you all right?"

"Yes, but Mom, could you leave, please? I need some time alone." My mom left my room.

God, I'm in a black pit and can't see light in any direction. How do I break these bonds? How do I break this addiction? I pray and pray, yet You don't seem to hear my cry. The Israelites waited four hundred years before You released them from bondage in Egypt. How long do I have to wait? Why won't You answer me?

A few hours later I left my room and discovered that I had the house to myself. Immediately my mouth went dry, and I looked at the computer sitting there, luring me.

Nobody will see.

I booted up and connected to the Internet. A Christian home page came up, and I stared at it for a minute. Then, hating myself for doing it, I logged on to the Playboy site. I swallowed hard as lewd photos filled the screen. A few minutes later, I switched back to the Christian web site. Five words stared at me:

Jesus watches where you surf.

A pair of eyes followed my cursor as I moved it across the screen. The words...the eyes...it was all too much. I fell across the keyboard, sobbing. "I'm a Christian who looks at porn sites! Forgive me and change me! Work something awesome in my life!"

The words on that screen still burned in my mind as I walked up the hill at church camp a few days later. I saw three girls playing Ping-Pong and introduced myself to them. As we talked, I noticed that a light seemed to radiate from them. Their smiles, their attitudes, their words—it was the glow of Jesus in them. At that moment, a warmth and love filled and satisfied me more than any lewd images ever had.

With sudden clarity I understood that pornography had controlled me because I'd tried to use it to fill a void for real love—the kind that only Jesus could fill. I found a spot alone and rededicated my life to Him. Once again, I asked God to forgive my sin and give me the strength to resist.

When I got home from camp, the first thing I saw when I walked in the house was the computer. Cold fear gripped me—my mouth went dry; my hands felt clammy. It was time to confront the monster in my life. Romans 6:17 came to my mind: "But thanks be to God that, though you used to be slaves to sin, you wholeheartedly obeyed the form of teaching to which you were entrusted." I prayed, then turned—and walked away.

That wasn't the only time I had to resist the temptation. In the months that followed, every time I turned on the computer I had to resist the temptation. Months passed, but finally, with God's help, the day came when it wasn't a struggle anymore.

God not only delivered me from my addiction, but He also gave me the tools to help other people break free from the shackles of sin.

Mark Moore

GOD LINKS

Have you been praying and praying for your friend, parent, or school without seeing an inch of change? Are you weary and tempted to give up? Then remember what Jesus said in Matthew 7:7. He said we're to ask, seek, and knock. He wasn't suggesting a one time "Please God, do this.…" He said to *keep on* asking, to *keep on* seeking, and to *keep on* knocking— in other words, to pray persistently!

A good way to remember to persevere and keep praying is **PUSH**:

Pray

Until

Something

Happens

Rejection

When I entered the seventh grade, romance was in the air and everyone I knew was pairing off into couples. Everyone, it seemed, except me. None of the girls seemed interested in me. Feeling rejected, I thought, *Okay, I guess I'll try guys.* And the guys I sought out *were* interested in me.

From that day forward, at age twelve, I became sexually active in the gay lifestyle. I still went to church and was really involved in my youth group. Everywhere I turned, from the pulpit and from my youth pastor, I heard that homosexuality was wrong. But honestly, I believed that since I didn't have a girlfriend, God didn't mind if I was gay.

Bad move.

I had no idea when I chose that path that it would eventually affect every area of my life. After four years, I was miserable and in turmoil. One night I decided to pray about my lifestyle. I simply asked, *Hey, is this all right? I mean, I feel guilty when I'm doing these things, but I still don't know if it's wrong or right.*

I guess God had been waiting four long years for me to ask that question, and He answered at the speed of light. *No, it's not okay.* I was shocked. I'd justified my actions for so long that I had somehow convinced myself that God would justify my life as well.

But He didn't. God clearly showed me that the way I had been living was wrong.

I was in for an even bigger shock when I discovered that to change my sexual lifestyle, I had to change my whole life! I had to change what I thought. I had to change how I acted. I had to change my friends. I didn't know if I could do it, and worse, if I could ever be free of the consequences of the terrible choices of a twelve-year-old.

I knew I needed God's help in a huge way, so I started my new life by spending time in prayer. I also started reading my Bible and talking to wise people. I had to work on changing my choices, which included giving up pornography and staying away from friends who might be bad influences on me. I won't kid you—it wasn't easy. But after I made those difficult choices, I made new friends and grew closer to the people in my youth group. And God really blessed me.

Yes, I made a poor decision when I was twelve. But when I turned to God, He showed me that homosexuality is not a physical disease or a physiological disorder. It's a disease of the heart, mind, and soul—and it is totally *reversible*. If you are struggling with this sin—or any sin—give God all your guilt and shame and ask Him in prayer to help you change your ways.

Life's a lot better without sin and shame. A whole lot better.

Jake Kilmon

10 iF YOU FEEL ALONE...

Young people around the world are leading
the way in a prayer revolution.
They're seeing God do miracles.

Bruce Wilkinson

Never Alone

I was nineteen years old when God dropped the idea of a mission tour in my heart. I wanted to tour the country with great music and simple teachings from God's Word that would be presented in a way teens could understand and apply. Of course, planning, financing, and carrying out a tour like this was way over my head, and I wondered who God had in mind to plan and execute it.

I was stunned to learn who God planned to use...*me*.

I'd never done anything like this in my life and hardly knew where to start. I began by contacting recording artists like Prodigal Soldiers/Prodigal Sonz, Pettidee, Jah Word,

Easop, and Marod, inviting them to join the "Make a Change" tour.

I chose the cities and sites where they would perform and made connections with churches, Fellowship of Christian Athletes chapters, Youth for Christ, and other youth ministries. Everything was in place except one small detail.

I had no money.

I didn't need just a few dollars. I needed a miracle— thousands of dollars to pay for the tour bus, food, gas, sound system, and artists' wages. The clock was ticking, and my pockets were empty. The first artist was scheduled to arrive in town, and I didn't have any of the money I needed for the tour, which was supposed to start that day.

Desperate, I fell on the floor of my bedroom and cried out to God for help. I prayed and prayed, telling God what I needed, but nothing changed. Finally exhausted, I lay in silence—listening.

After a while, I heard that quiet voice of the Holy Spirit give me the name of a friend on the West Coast. I called him and told him about the tour. He wired me the five thousand dollars I needed on the spot.

God came through with the finances, but that doesn't mean the rest was smooth sailing. I'd never driven a bus, yet I was the bus driver for the tour group. I drove so many miles that each city became a blur to me. We ministered all day; then I drove all night. I was way past exhausted and I felt so alone.

I was driving the last leg of the trip between San Diego and Atlanta alone in the bus when I felt the presence of God so intensely that I began to weep.

I looked to my right and said, "Holy Spirit, what is Your purpose?"

The four words God spoke changed my life.

I'm here for you.

God was here for me. *Me!* I was not alone. God had been with me every time we stopped for food. He'd provided money every time we stopped for gas. He'd been beside me, keeping me awake during all those lonely miles.

God provided five thousand dollars in a miraculous way.

Thousands of youth across the nation were touched by Jesus on that trip, but the biggest change may have been in me. No matter where I go or what I do for the rest of my life, I'll never forget those words.

I'm here for you.

And He'll be there for you as well.

Tywone Thomas

GOD LINKS

the most important thing

You don't have to experience some kind of crisis or disaster to express your love for God. Jesus said in Mark 12:30 that the most important thing is to love the Lord our God with all of our hearts. That means that the central focus of our relationship with God is to love Him with everything that's in us! Expressing our love to God is a powerful thing.

- Today, practice loving God and wrapping your entire life around Him all day. As you walk down your high school hallway, say, "I love You, Lord!" Whisper it during algebra class: "I love You, Lord!" Repeat it during lunchtime or at soccer practice: "I love You, Lord!"

- Write Mark 12:30 on an index card, carry it with you, and memorize it. Then go out and love the Lord today.

I'm Loved

My hands shook as I felt the cold, heavy metal of my father's gun. I tried to imagine what the world would be like without me. At first I pictured everyone crying and wishing they'd been nice to me. Then I imagined that no one would care at all—that they'd only laugh. Part of me wanted to pull the trigger, but another part of me was afraid. *How did I ever get to this point?*

I'd been raised in church, and I gave my life to Jesus when I was five, but it just seemed like the thing to do. I didn't understand what I was doing. My family was strict. I was taught never to speak unless spoken to. I wasn't to ask for anything or take anything that was offered. I was to love others and put them before myself. My purpose in life was to make everyone feel better. But the more I tried to do that, the worse I felt. Fear wrapped itself around me, and after a while I became afraid of everyone.

I gave my toys to other kids so they would like me, but I always felt alone. As I got older, I craved an unconditional kind of love that I had never experienced. In middle school, I thought I might find that kind of love from boys, but I was always afraid.

When I was in the seventh grade, I attended a dance. I don't know what happened—the mood and music seemed to make me brave. I saw a guy sitting all alone and mustered up the courage to ask him to dance.

He refused.

And something inside me snapped. All the rejection and hurt I'd held inside me since I was a child exploded. I burst into tears and ran home. Then I found my father's gun. I intended to put a bullet in my brain and end the suffering, but I couldn't even do that right.

That night I crawled into bed and, miserable and tired of my own thoughts, turned on a Christian talk radio program. I stared out the window half listening to what they said. Then I fell on my face screaming for God to rescue me.

"God save me!" I screamed. "I need You!"

Suddenly I felt the most incredible love begin to wash over me in waves. I had never imagined that such a love existed. It was so powerful and intense that I didn't think I could take anymore, but another wave came...and another. I didn't know anyone could be loved the way I felt loved at that moment. Something like a warm blanket of comfort wrapped itself around me, and I knew that I was connected to God in a way I had never been before.

When I woke up the next morning, I knew immediately that something was different. Then a smile spread across my face as I remembered.

Oh yeah, I'm loved.

Melinda Spear

Home at Last

For Christmas the year I turned twelve, an officer took me from my home to the police station because my mom couldn't take care of me. I'd gotten pretty good at taking care of myself. So, I spent Christmas in a court-ordered emergency-care shelter. After that I went into foster care. From there I went to a group home. Finally, they shipped me across the country to the East Coast. All those experiences confirmed what I'd suspected since I was a little girl: I was the kid nobody wanted.

After graduating from high school, I ran away and went back to California. I don't know what I thought I would find there, but I certainly didn't find a long-lost family to greet me with open arms. I never really knew my parents, and no matter where I lived I felt alone and incomplete. I attempted suicide a few times because I wanted to die and go home to God.

Home. That had a nice ring to it. I figured if I died, I would finally have a home—and the pain would stop. But I survived my attempts at suicide. And I was surviving the best I could when I agreed to go with my church to Covelo, an Indian reservation. While we were there, I saw people who'd been persecuted and broken for centuries—and they had survived.

On the last day of the trip, the beautiful Indian woman who'd cooked for us all week gave her life to Jesus. I watched as she was baptized in the river. She prayed to God, received a blessing, and was submerged in the blue-green water. Seconds passed...then she shot up out of the water with such joy!

Watching that baptism, I finally understood what the Lord had been trying to show me all along. Christianity isn't just about dying and going to heaven.

It's about dying to our old lives and living a new life as a new person.

I didn't have to kill myself! I had *to die to myself!*

I wanted that joyous new beginning.

Right then, the Lord spoke to me and said, *I will be a friend that sticks closer than a brother. You'll never be alone, for I am with you. When your parents forsake you, I will be your Daddy.* I was so shocked that God cared so much for *me* that I cried for a long time.

I didn't have to die to be at home with God! The next morning I opened my eyes and said, "Good morning, Daddy." Then I talked to Him as though He was right there with me—and He was! When I was in the car, He was with me. When I went shopping, He showed me people who needed encouragement or just a hug. I never knew God had so much to say.

I can't say that the rest of my life has been rosy. I lost my job—but God helped me. As I was riding my bike down the street one day, I was hit by a car, but God healed me. He also sent people from the church to help me.

Today I have a great job, a car, and a scholarship to college.

The best part is that I'm finally home—in God's loving arms.

Marie Claire Facio

11 if GOD says "PRAY!" ...

Prayer begins by talking to God,
but it ends by listening to Him.

Fulton J. Sheen

Sisters

It was a rainy, dreary day in Russia, where I'd traveled with Teen Mania to work with orphans in a children's camp. After we performed a drama called "Ragman" for the children, they huddled around us on the front porch of the barracks where they lived. Our leader, with the help of a translator, explained how much God loved each one of them and about how Jesus had died for them.

"Would any of you like to give your lives to Jesus?" the leader asked.

Several children responded to the message by asking for prayer. But Sasha, the child curled up in my lap, did not. I hardly knew the little girl, but I wanted to leave her with the gift that would change not only her life, but also her eternity. I was so burdened that I prayed quietly while I held her.

"Please, God, work in Sasha's heart," I prayed. "Show her that even though she has no relationship with a mother and father here on earth, You are her Father and will never leave her."

No sooner had I prayed those words than Sasha jumped out of my lap and tugged on my hand. She pulled me forward to the translator. I went over the plan of salvation and tried to help her understand how important this decision was. Sasha nodded and said she understood. She wanted to give her life to Jesus.

I led her in a prayer of commitment, and when we'd finished praying, I looked up to see Sasha weeping. She looked at me with tear-stained cheeks and said in Russian, "Now I have a Father. And we are *sisters*—you and I—*forever!*"

I got down on my knees and held my little sister in my arms.

Through Sasha, I learned to see Christians not as individual children of God, but as His family. It was hard to leave her behind in Russia, but I will never forget my sister, Sasha.

And I am grateful that I will have eternity to shower her with a sister's love.

Michelle Epperly

Colorado Dreaming

It was a bright, sunny Colorado afternoon—the last way I wanted to spend it was sitting in a dentist's chair. But the appointment had been made, and I had to go. My dad and I didn't say much as he drove me there. When he stopped in front of the dentist's office, he told me he was going to run some errands.

"Bye—love you. See you in an hour." I stepped out of the car.

I looked through magazines in the waiting room until they called my name. A nurse ushered me to the dental chair, and I lay back and let my mind wander to a special track practice I would be attending the next day. Suddenly, I felt an uneasiness about my dad and a strong urge to pray for him.

This is ridiculous, I thought. *I just saw Dad.*

I tried to concentrate on my track practice, but I couldn't get my mind off my dad. The urge to pray grew stronger—but I didn't even know *what* to pray about. But I couldn't think about anything else. Finally, I prayed.

Lord, thank You for my dad, I began. *Thank You that he is in Your hands and that Your Spirit rests upon him. I ask that You protect him and keep him safe.* I continued to pray for a few minutes. Then my mind wandered to something else. By the time Dad met me out front, I'd forgotten all about the prayer.

"The strangest thing happened while I was running

errands," he said, as he pulled into traffic. "I was at a stop-light at the busiest intersection in town when—well, I guess I fell asleep. The car was in gear and rolled into traffic. All of a sudden something jerked me awake, and I opened my eyes just in time to see that I was seconds from a head-on collision with a semi. I slammed on the brakes and swerved out of his way."

Chills rippled down my neck as I remembered how close I came to not praying.

I love both my dad and my heavenly Father.

And I'm so grateful that, for a moment that beautiful afternoon, my prayer connected one to the other and kept my dad out of harm's way.

Sarah Mathis

GOD LINKS

How can we "pray without ceasing" as Paul instructed in 1 Thessalonians 5:17?

Send up "arrow prayers" to God all day long.

As you turn to the Lord throughout the day, a constant conversation develops. "Help me, Lord" or "Bless my classmate, Jesus" or "Thank You!" whispered, spoken aloud, thought, or sung. Arrow prayers help you stay tuned in to God no matter what you're doing. They help keep your channel to God open and allow you to hear Him when His Spirit calls you to pray for a pressing need, just as He did with Sarah. Try shooting your prayers all day to the God who is listening!

Let everything around you be a visual cue to pray.

If you see a Handicap Parking sign in the parking lot, pray for the students with disabilities at your school. When you pass other high schools, pray for the salvation of all the students and teachers there.

Ongoing prayers like these can bring joy and a deeper awareness of God's presence in your everyday life.

Pray!

Night after night, sixteen-year-old Laura March lay in bed, unable to sleep because of the burden God had given her for her high school—especially for the FCA (Fellowship of Christian Athletes), a group she'd been part of since her freshman year. So much excitement would well up in her heart about what God was going to do that she couldn't get to sleep, so she'd pray until she did.

Lord, keep Your hand over our whole FCA group, especially the leaders, so that everything we do is God-breathed and not our own human plans. And let many students be saved this year!

One night that summer she almost bolted out of bed after hearing one word: "Pray!"

Oh, Lord. I'm tired. It's 2:00 A.M., and I've got to be at my summer job by 8:00 in the morning. All I want to do is sleep!

But the Spirit urged her: *You've got to pray. Pray for FCA. Pray for friends. Pray for your school.*

She slipped to her knees and began to intercede.

When school started in September, Laura met with the other leaders of FCA. It had always been a nice group, but not a very spiritual one. It was more social and was dominated by the "popular" kids; a place to hang out and have a good time together, but not a place where any lives were really changed or souls saved.

As Laura and the other leaders talked, she discovered they wanted God to do something different that year too, and together they prayed earnestly that every plan and word would be God's and that He'd bring a spiritual awakening among the students who came to their meetings.

Give an altar call, they sensed God saying. But this only happened at midyear or at special outreach events.

That night would be the first meeting.

Laura's friend, Jolene, gave the lesson, followed with an altar call. Six students immediately gave their lives to Jesus. At their meeting the following week, twelve students said "Yes!" to God for the first time, and the week after, three more students were transformed by the power of God. That made twenty-one new believers—more than they'd seen in years. During that year, God worked in the lives of many teens, and by the end of the term, the FCA group was forty strong and was growing and emphasizing outreach and evangelism instead of popularity.

All because somebody responded when God said, "Pray!"

12 if YOU'RE DESPERATE...

> Every chain that spirits wear
> crumbles in the breath of prayer.

John Greenleaf Whittier

Secrets

I don't know if all families have secrets, but mine had a closet full of them. I didn't feel loved and protected in the family I grew up in. My father sexually abused me for years, until I reached an age when I could refuse to see him. But ending the abuse wasn't the same as ending the experience. It went on and on and on—in my memory.

The memories were like a scary closet: If the door cracked open even a little, horrible things would jump out. I tried to put the memories out of my mind, but they wouldn't go away. They haunted me day and night.

I attended a youth event one night, and right in the

middle of the drama, that closet door opened. I was so over-whelmed with pain that I began to cry. I kept feeling like I should ask for prayer, but it's not easy to tell secrets you've held tightly for so long. But the need for release overcame the nauseating thought of telling someone what had happened. Finally, during the altar call, I went forward for prayer.

While someone prayed for me, I cried out to God from the depths of my soul, *Lord, I don't want to remember anymore!*

It wasn't until later that I realized God had performed a miracle. I couldn't remember the pain. All the agony was gone.

God didn't just put a lock on that closet and leave those memories inside clamoring to get out. He actually opened the door and made them leave.

The closet is empty—there are no scary memories to haunt me.

Ron Williamson

GOD LINKS

God gives us a wonderful promise in Jeremiah 33:3. Think of this verse as *God's Private Telephone Number— JE:333*. In it the Lord says:

> Call to Me, and I will answer you, and
> show you great and mighty things,
> which you do not know.
>
> **N K J V**

This direct hot line to heaven is available any time of night or day, and He'll never put you on hold or send you to His voice mail. And He doesn't just listen—He wants to speak to you and show you things you *need to know*, beginning with His amazing, unconditional love.

Outcast

When I started fifth grade, I was bused to an inner-city school. I did everything I could to fit in, but I wasn't considered smart, pretty, or popular. It was bad enough to feel like an outcast, but the other kids seemed to find some kind of weird pleasure in picking on me. Even the few people I considered friends put me down.

The harassment lasted all the way through junior high, and by the time I turned fourteen, I was seriously depressed. My parents were Christians and went to church regularly, but none of that seemed real to me. My reality was that I was ugly, a nerd, and weird.

The summer before ninth grade I didn't feel like I could take it anymore, so I tried to kill myself. God must have been watching out for me, because I survived. After that difficult time, I attended summer camp and felt the Holy Spirit urge me to open up about my depression.

Finally, I blurted it out to my best friend and her mother. Then I told my own parents how I felt. But the most important step I took was asking God to take over my life. I figured He couldn't do any worse than I'd done with it.

I began talking to God and being real about how I felt. "God," I said, "I'm tired of living like this. Seriously, I just want to die because the pain I feel is so bad. You said that everything You created is good, so why do I feel so ugly? I want to feel loved. Help me, God!"

When I started praying, I expected my feelings of ugliness to just go away. And when they didn't, I seriously doubted my salvation. But what else could I do? I hated myself. So while I prayed to God, I listened to all the mean, hateful things that had been said about me for so long. And I listened to myself—I even rejected myself!

I stayed on an emotional roller coaster until my junior year in high school. Then one morning my mom said, "Shana, I'm tired of walking on egg shells around you. You tell me that you love and trust God. You tell me that He is perfect and holy. Then you turn around and call Him a liar by saying that you're ugly and worthless. You need to ask God what He has to say about you. Then you need to decide if you believe God or not. Either He's truthful or He's a liar. He can't be both."

Wow. That made me think—hard. I asked God what He thought about me. First He told me that He loved me and that He had plans for my life. Then He said, *When I created you, I stepped back and said, "That's good." I didn't step back and say, "Oops, I messed up."*

Those words began to sink in, and I listened to them rather than to all the negative self-talk and the memories of cruel words. And guess what? The depression I'd battled for so long—lifted!

God had always accepted me.

And now I accept myself.

Shana Daniels

Learning to Trust Again

My dad was a drug addict, and my mother divorced him before I was born. When I was four years old, she married my stepfather. He was really the only dad I ever knew. That's why it was so terrifying when he raped me. And it didn't happen just once—he forced himself on me again and again. And when I resisted, he beat me.

I'd been raised in church and taught to pray. Every time I heard his footsteps coming toward me I prayed, *God, make him stop!* But he didn't stop. He wouldn't stop. Not only did he hurt me physically, but he also changed who I believed I was. He convinced me that I was not worthy of love—that I deserved what he did to me.

In the deepest part of my soul I believed that I was unlovable. My real father didn't love me enough to get off drugs. My stepfather didn't love me enough to stop hurting me. I guess I felt like God didn't love me enough to make the hurting end.

But that didn't stop me from praying. Prayer was the only hope I had.

By the time I was eleven, my mom figured out that I was very unhappy and took me to the church therapist. And somehow, the whole ugly story came out. After that day, my stepfather never hurt me again because he was no longer in our lives.

But having the sexual abuse stop didn't make me whole

again. I felt so unlovable that I didn't want to live. I tried to commit suicide and was admitted to a mental hospital several times. Even then, I continued to ask God for help.

I didn't experience some kind of lightning strike that wiped out all the hurt I'd endured, but God *did* help me. He brought me friends who loved me and weren't afraid to show it. He taught me how to trust again. He told me that I was put on earth for a reason. Most of all, He told me over and over how much He loved me.

And eventually I started to like myself.

My suicidal days are over. Instead of dying, I want to live a long time. Why wouldn't I? My Father loves me.

Cari Newton

GOD LINKS

spicing up your
prayer life

No matter what you're going through, seeking God for a closer walk and a deeper intimacy with Him can renew your heart. If you need some direction as you pray, try these tips:

S: Silence. Try listening more than speaking. King David often said that he waited upon God. When we are silent, God has the greatest chance to speak to us.

P: Practice the presence of God. We can take advantage of many moments during the day to enter into God's presence. Turn off the radio as you drive to school or work and get in God's presence, talk to God while you mow the lawn, or pray from a list of prayer requests you've hung in your bathroom.

I: Intercede for others more often than you pray for your own needs. This takes your focus off yourself and onto what the Lord wants to do through you.

C: Confession. There is nothing like confession to draw your heart near to God. Real humility will lead you into His presence more quickly than anything else. The Bible says, "God opposes the proud, but gives grace to the humble" (James 4:6). Make confession a regular part of your prayer time.

E: Enter into a prayer covenant with at least one other person. People who are serious about prayer enter a battlefield, and they can't do it alone and expect to survive very long. Meet regularly with a prayer partner and pray with and for each other.

(Adapted from Kevin Young's "Spice Up Your Prayer Life" at The Coaching Center, www.gocampus.org.)

13 iF YOU KEEP ON PRAYING...

**You can take prayer out of schools,
but you can't take praying students out!**

Mike Higgs

Leading a Rebellion

In 1962 the U.S. Supreme Court voted to remove prayer from American classrooms. I knew that as a fact of history, but in my small town in Texas, it wasn't a fact of life. In my hometown, everybody knew everybody and most people were raised in church. We continued to pray at football games and other public events, and it was never a problem. At least not until my junior year, when the school board decided to enforce the law. They passed an ordinance prohibiting the prayer that was spoken over the loudspeaker before every football game.

Once that happened, people also began to question the

legality of the campus ministry that met every morning for prayer and once a week during lunch. Like many in the student body, I was shocked at the changes. As president of the campus ministry, I found myself in the middle of the biggest spiritual battle I'd ever encountered.

I went to the superintendent, who was also a Christian. "Why is this happening? What can we do about it?"

"I'm sorry. There's nothing I can do," he said. "If anything changes, it will have to be you students who take action."

But we're just a bunch of teens! I thought. *What can we possibly do?*

Since no one in an authority position in our school would help, I decided to go over their heads—straight to God. I prayed fervently for His wisdom. He asked me what biblical example I could follow. I took a hard look at what people in the Bible did when they were forbidden by law to worship God, and I discovered something amazing—they worshiped anyway!

I gathered a group of students, and we began to pray that God would help us fight just like those in the Bible had done. Still, we were clueless about what to do. One student's father presented a plan to the school board that would provide a way for us to pray, and it had huge support in the community.

But the school board rejected it.

Then God gave us an idea that was risky, but we weren't about to give up. At the next football game, as fans filled the stadium, we all took our places. Since the law had been enforced, instead of prayer, the stadium now had a moment of silence before the football game.

But instead of obeying the silent rule, our group began saying the Lord's Prayer out loud. Then the most unexpected thing happened. The student body joined. Parents joined. Children joined. Teachers and faculty joined. The prayer spread like wildfire across the stadium. Even the fans on the opposing team joined in our act of rebellion!

The moment we said "Amen," the stadium exploded into applause and cheering.

And later the school board approved a plan allowing us to pray. At games after that amazing night, a standing ovation followed the opening prayer.

Elizabeth Cartwright

GOD LINKS

God can use prayer walks around your high school campus in a powerful way. Here are some suggestions:

— On a weekly or monthly basis, gather thirty minutes or an hour before school starts.

— Form groups of two or three and walk and pray around the perimeter of your campus (Jericho-style), in the hallways, and at each classroom.

— Have each person write Scriptures on note cards to take on the prayer walk.

— Remember the three Ws as you prayer-walk:

Welcome:
Invite God's Spirit to come and move.

Worship:
Glorify God in that place, even if it's just in your heart. Focus on Him!

Warfare:
Fight for the people you are praying for with God's spiritual resources and thank Him for the mighty weapons He gives through prayer.

Encourage prayer-walkers to target their prayers. For example, one group could pray for leadership, one for the football team, one for teachers, and one for spiritual awakening.

A faith That wouldn't Die

Rachel Packard didn't see the world—or even her high school—the way most people did. Most people saw the stark reality: Her school was more like a war zone than a safe place to learn. Drug deals went down in the parking lot, behind the cafeteria, and in the halls. Violence broke out on campus, and gangs bullied and terrorized the students.

Most people saw a bunch of bad kids.

Rachel saw a lot of hurting people.

She'd become a Christian at an early age and wanted everyone to know Jesus. After all, if you have a best friend, it's only natural to want to introduce Him to others, especially if they are in pain and need help. The violence, drugs, and gangs drove Rachel straight to God. She prayed for their salvation, healing, and peace.

During her freshman year, Rachel lost her appetite. Weakness and fatigue plagued her. A trip to the doctor confirmed the worst: Rachel had leukemia.

"I don't know how long I'm going to live," Rachel told her parents, "but I'm committed to making every day count for Jesus while I'm on earth." Every day she asked them to pray over her that God would give her divine appointments with classmates. And Rachel began praying that every student in her school would come to know Jesus.

As news of Rachel's cancer spread, the students and faculty watched her to see how she would handle it. Instead of depression and despair, they saw joy and peace in her eyes and her countenance. Frankly, they were baffled. If anyone had the right to be bitter, angry, or withdrawn, Rachel did. It became obvious that Rachel had a source of strength that most of them had never seen or known. She seemed more concerned about *them* than about herself.

Over the next three years, Rachel endured chemotherapy, radiation, and every treatment medical science had to offer, yet her health deteriorated. One day she told her parents, "I'm ready to go home and be with Jesus now, but I want my high school to spend eternity in heaven with me." That night, she wrote a letter addressed to all the students at her school.

A few weeks later, Rachel died and her mother asked the principal if her daughter's classmates could come to her funeral and listen to a letter Rachel had written them. Hundreds of students asked permission to attend, and the principal arranged for a fleet of buses to take them.

During the service the pastor read Rachel's letter. "Dear classmates, I told my parents that I was willing to die and go home to eternity if I could bring all of you with me. My Savior made a way for you to get to the other side...."

As soon he finished reading the letter, the pastor looked up and asked, "How many of you want to see Rachel some-day on the other side of eternity?" Almost all the students surged forward and gave their lives to Jesus. Others rededicated their lives to Him.

For three years, Rachel had prayed for her schoolmates, and on the day of her funeral she reaped a harvest of souls for eternity.

She had a faith that wouldn't die.

from Bullets to Baptism

When I first learned the prayer of Jabez, "Lord, bless me indeed and expand my territory," I wondered how much God could expand the territory of a teenager from Yorktown, Virginia. I mean, there's only so much a teenager can do, right?

Eventually, I became one of forty other teens from Yorktown who prayed the prayer of Jabez every day. We weren't asking for personal gain as much as saying to God, *We feel inadequate, but You're adequate! Expand what we can do as an outreach.*

Then we got news that a little congregation in Philadelphia was asking God for help in reaching inner-city kids. Youth groups from Florida and Michigan combined forces to try to help, and we joined them. The plan was to put on a game show and skits in the inner city. We would share God's love in parks, on the streets, and in housing projects.

It sounded great when we were in Yorktown making preparations. But reality hit us right between the eyes the night before the outreach when a guy was shot on the street where we were supposed to minister. I'll be honest—we were scared.

We walked through the streets of Philadelphia's inner city, picking up bullets and inviting people to attend the game show. And they came! Over four days, with the combined efforts of four churches, 888 people gave their lives to Jesus. That's definitely God's form of multiplication. Life for those people was never the same. And neither were the lives of some of us from Yorktown.

God blessed us *indeed!*

Sean Wood

GOD LINKS

And Jabez called on the God of Israel
saying, "Oh, that You would bless me indeed,
and enlarge my territory, that Your hand
would be with me, and that You would keep
me from evil, that I may not cause pain." So
God granted him what he requested.

1 Chronicles 4:10, NKJV

Incorporate praying the prayer of Jabez into your life
for thirty days and see what God does. Pray it as a
youth group before outreaches and mission trips. Pray
it as a Bible club or prayer group, and pray it
individually. And get ready for things to happen! The
four requests are:

1.

Please bless me indeed. (*Indeed* means *a lot!*)

2.

Please enlarge my territory by expanding my
influence and what I can do for Your Kingdom.

3.

Please put Your hand on me!

4.

Please keep me from evil!

14 if YOU STRUGGLE iN YOUR FAITH...

Prayer is no fitful, short-lived thing.
It is no voice crying unheard and
unheeded in the silence.
It is a voice that goes into God's ear.

E. M. Bounds

A crippled soul

Life was rough for Andrey Valuy, a child who lived in Belarus. The collapse of the Soviet Union had swung open the door to a new lawlessness, which arrived in the form of the Russian mafia. And while the economy was plunging, crime was at an all-time high. Andrey watched from the sidelines as an American group of teenagers performed a drama in the village square.

After the American teens were done performing, Andrey saw a man run up to the group carrying his five-year-old son, who was crippled. "Can your God heal my son's leg?" he called out in Russian. Interpreters translated the request to the

American teens, and they gathered around the boy and prayed.

Nothing happened.

They prayed more, but still nothing happened.

Suddenly the leader of the American group looked up and stared directly at Andrey. "God wants *you* to pray for this child," he said.

"Me?" Andrey gasped. "Why me?"

"Because God said you were the one to do it."

"How?"

Through a translator, the man gave Andrey simple instructions. "Just put your hand on the boy, and ask the Lord to heal his leg. Then talk to the Lord like you'd talk to me."

Andrey stood frozen in place. The last thing he wanted was for his friends to make fun of him. Still, the Americans had given him candy and been kind to him; this particular missionary was staying in his home. He rested a tentative hand on the boy's leg and whispered a short prayer in the boy's ear, talking to God as he might talk to one of his friends. Then he stepped back and watched the boy.

Nothing.

Andrey turned to leave with one last glance back. A wide smile spread across the boy's face as he took first one stumbling step and then another. He walked awkwardly to the nearby bench—then ran across the square, laughing all the way.

The boy's father put his hands to his face and cried out while the crowd watched in amazement as the boy ran. For days afterward, all Andrey could think about was that God had used *him* to heal a crippled boy.

But eventually the American teens left Belarus, and life returned to normal. Like most boys his age, Andrey skipped school and lived on the streets from sunrise to sunset. Sometimes he played with his friends. Sometimes he washed cars in the hotel parking lot. Sometimes foreigners gave him money. But the Russian mafia paid in drugs—first marijuana and hashish, then stronger and more dangerous drugs.

And what started out for Andrey as harmless experimentation turned into addiction. By the time he was sixteen, Andrey's life revolved around cigarettes, alcohol, and drugs. No one could penetrate the darkness in his soul. Nothing mattered to him.

Nothing…except the memory of that child laughing and running around the square, his crippled legs healed. One night, Andrey fell on his knees and cried out to that same God for a miracle. And the same Jesus who healed crippled legs now healed Andrey's crippled soul. Andrey Valuy rose from his knees a new creature in Christ Jesus.

The power alcohol and drugs had in his life was broken, and Andrey started his life anew. He traveled to Norway for discipleship training. After his training he ministered in Nepal for two months. And when back in Belarus, Andrey spoke to a crowd of a thousand people, and many gave their lives to Jesus. Today he takes the good news of a miracle-working God around the world.

friends in High places

I was a happy girl who loved Jesus with all my heart—until I outgrew Him, the same way you eventually outgrow the Easter bunny and the tooth fairy. I packed away all three along with my childhood memories. Now I had more important things to think about. I wanted new friends— friends that were popular.

I tried talking to the kids who were in the right social circles, but they didn't seem to notice that I was alive. I tried dressing like them. I tried hanging out where they hung out. When none of those things worked, I felt desperate.

I finally realized that I would do *anything* to be friends with those people.

So I tried giving people money—that really got their attention!—and they became my friends. I tried delivering juicy morsels of gossip—some people hung around me so they'd know what was happening. Drinking seemed to make me popular with some people. I still felt invisible to guys, but when I offered to have sex with them, I was their friend! I was so thrilled to finally have friends that I did whatever they wanted. If my friend wanted something she couldn't afford, I stole it for her.

Every Sunday morning I walked into church as though nothing in me had changed, but inside I felt awful. I wanted to live differently, but my new friends were too important to me. So I made up lies to stay in the center of the crowd. My social life had become more important than my conscience.

After eight months of this life, things changed: I ran out

of money to give my friends. I ran out of gossip and I ran out of lies. Without the lies, money, alcohol, sex, and gossip—my friends vanished like the stars at dawn. I was alone again—only this time I was alone and sad and disgusted with myself as well. I was so miserable that I blew the dust off my Bible and actually spoke to God. "Lord, I'm tired," I said. "I repent of my sins and ask You to forgive me. And, God, could I please have a friend—a real friend?"

The instant I prayed that prayer, a burden seemed to lift from me. My heart felt a lightness I hadn't experienced in years. The next day I flipped open my Bible and stumbled across this passage:

> "Greater love has no one than this, than to lay down one's life for his friends. You are My friends if you do whatever I command you. No longer do I call you servants, for a servant does not know what his master is doing; but I have called you friends, for all things that I heard from My Father I have made known to you."
>
> **John 15:13-15, NKJV**

When I read that passage, I knew that I didn't need sex, drugs, alcohol, or any other destructive thing to find a friend. Jesus was the friend I'd wanted all along. Our relationship wasn't based on what I could do for Him. It was based on what He'd already done for me. He died for me! How could a friend do more?

I also read in the Bible that if we delight in Him, God will give us the desires of our hearts. And He did that for me. My greatest desire was for a friend and God granted that desire.

So what if my best friend heals the sick, raises the dead, and sits at the right hand of God in heaven? I always wanted friends in high places!

Gladys Donnel

GOD LINKS

When you pray God's Word, you can pray with confidence because you are asking in accordance with God's principles and His revealed will. Personalizing God's Word will also enlarge your prayer vocabulary. You can pray a verse for yourself, for others, or for a particular situation. Here's how to get started:

Memorize the Word

Personalize the Word

Pray the Word

Visualize the Word

Try praying these verses over the next five days,
one each day:

Romans 15:5-6; Luke 4:18-19; Psalm 34:7;
Jeremiah 1:5; Ephesians 6:9

15 iF YOU NEED A MIRACLE...

Prayer works miracles among men and brings to pass great things.

E. M. Bounds

African Adventure

The bus groaned to a stop in a small village outside Kumasi in Ghana, West Africa, in the summer of 1999, and I felt like groaning too. I looked around at the other members of the Teen Mania mission team and saw faces lined with fatigue as people stretched and stepped off the bus in our new location. We'd performed three to four dramas a day for nearly two weeks in addition to traveling. We were all homesick and tired.

As the nineteen-year-old leader of the group, it was my responsibility to ask the chief of the village, through an interpreter, for permission to perform.

He nodded his consent and everyone enthusiastically demonstrated the love of God to the villagers through drama and song. Afterward, I invited them to accept Jesus. The chief and village elders responded first; then others followed. I was about to lead them in prayer when a disturbance rippled through the crowd.

I saw an old man bent with age leaning on a gnarled walking stick. He moved slowly, and as he drew closer, I saw his milky white eyes and realized why the villagers had parted for him. He was blind.

A wave of compassion and faith washed over me. Without thinking, I announced, "God is going to heal this man! And it will be the power of Jesus that does it! Today you will see that God is real!"

No sooner had the words come out of my mouth than I thought, *Oh, no! What was I thinking? What came over me?*

I asked two of my teammates, Nick and Jessica, to lay their hands on the man's eyes and pray that God would restore his sight. We all prayed for several minutes and they moved their hands from his eyes.

Nothing.

Lord, I prayed, *I just told this whole crowd that Jesus was going to heal him, and nothing—absolutely nothing—happened. They're going to stone us or run us out of town!*

Another thought crossed my mind. "Nick, spit on the ground and make some mud."

"What?"

"Well...Jesus did it when He healed a blind man. Make some mud."

Nick got on his knees and spit in the dirt. I put the mud over the man's eyes and the three of us prayed again. This time when Nick and Jessica removed their hands, the man's eyes had cleared!

The old man stretched his hand to touch things he'd never seen before. The pastor from Ghana, who translated for us, waved his hand in front of the man's face. The old man grabbed his hand, and his face lit up with a smile.

Excitement moved through the crowd. Many men, women, and children accepted Jesus as Savior that day. They were eternally changed by the power of God.

And so were we.

Jeremy Meister

The Last Laugh

I felt a flush of embarrassment creep up my neck all the way to the roots of my hair. Instead of trying harder to play my part in the drama that my team was presenting to a little village in Kenya, I started laughing. I didn't laugh because it was funny; I laughed because I was so embarrassed. This was the last drama on the last day of our trip to Africa, and our performance was so bad that everyone—the audience, the translator, and even the team—had started laughing.

We were mortified.

And if that wasn't bad enough, afterward when our team leader, Lindsey, presented the gospel to the people, no one was interested in God. I felt horrible. *No wonder,* I thought grimly. *How could anyone take us seriously when we laughed the whole time? How could God use us when we were so awful?*

Lindsey pressed on, inviting anyone who needed healing to come forward. *Fat chance,* I thought, just as a young woman ran forward and threw a baby in Lindsey's arms. Violent convulsions shook the infant.

We all prayed while the baby's eyes rolled back in his head and the color drained from his face. Then, as we prayed, he stopped breathing. I was so desperate for God to do something—*anything*—that I almost stopped breathing too.

Minutes passed as the whole village watched us pray fervently. I'd never prayed so hard in my life, but God kept giving me words. I lost track of time and of everything around me except that baby. The situation seemed hopeless, yet I felt the comforting presence of God.

Then—a shuddering breath! And another! He was breathing!

An hour later, it seemed as though nothing had ever happened to him. His young mother was only fifteen years old. She explained to us through a translator that she was pregnant with a second child and was on her way to kill herself and the baby when she stopped to watch us. It wasn't until the baby appeared to be dead that she realized how desperately she wanted him to live.

She gave her life to Jesus that afternoon. I left Africa stunned that God would do such a miracle, saving three lives, when we had represented Him so poorly.

Then I remembered: It isn't about how good *we* are.

It's all about how good *He* is.

Michel Price

The pink sari

I was sixteen years old, and I was so nervous about my first mission trip to India that I read everything I could find on the nation to try to prepare myself. I read about Hinduism so I could understand the Hindus' religious background. I even found a Christian web site that reported on the Christian church in India. I discovered that the people were so hungry for spiritual peace that they would sacrifice almost anything to find it.

I became so burdened for the people of India that every morning at sunrise I prayed for them. One morning during prayer the Lord opened my spiritual eyes and allowed me to see a sea of brown faces. Then one face came sharply into focus. It was a teenage girl about my age with long black hair hanging in a braid down her back. She was about my height and wore a pink sari with burgundy roses woven into the material. She looked right at me and wept.

I didn't understand what I'd seen, but I thought the girl might represent the people of India, so I prayed for her. After this vision, as I tried to keep up with class assignments and prepare for the trip, I forgot all about her.

Two months later I traveled with Teen Mania to India. As soon as we entered one particular village, I felt the tension between the Hindu and Muslim villagers who stood on opposite sides of the square. The Hindu priestess watched us with such cold hostility that my stomach tied itself in knots.

I somehow made it through the drama we performed for the villagers, and when we were done, I scanned the crowd. I almost gasped aloud when I saw a familiar face. It was the same girl from my vision, with a long black braid hanging down her back, and she was wearing a pink sari with burgundy roses. She sat by the side of the road with her mother.

I grabbed a few of my teammates and hurried over to the girl. Through a translator, I learned that both the girl and her mother were former Muslims who'd converted to Christianity.

Oh, they already know God, I thought with a sense of disappointment. *I wonder why God showed me her face—weeping?* I asked if there was anything we could pray about. The girl didn't answer me.

"Can we just pray and ask God to bless you?" I asked.

The translator turned to me and said, "This girl had polio, which left her paralyzed in her left leg. She can't move it. And she wants to be healed."

She's crippled! I kneeled down in front of her and placed my hand on her leg. "Lord, Your Word says that by Your wounds we are made whole," I prayed. "This girl is your child, so by Your word she can be made whole. Thank You for the blood of Jesus that cleanses her and heals her."

Nothing happened.

I had no idea what to do so I just continued to pray quietly. Then I sensed God telling me to pray specifically that the girl's bones would be made new. A deep urgency welled up in me and I said, "Lord, cause these bones to be made whole!" Suddenly the girl started making funny noises. I asked her to move her leg. Tears streaming down her face, she moved it in one direction and then the other. Then we helped her to stand.

I asked her to jump.

She jumped a little, then threw her arms around me, sobbing.

Both of us cried as we joined hands and danced around the square.

Those in the village who'd been hostile just moments before gathered around and said, "She was crippled, but now she's healed!"

Jeanette Beal

GOD LINKS

In the kind of world we live in, people are so concerned about "me, myself, and I" that they mostly pray about things that affect their own lives. But did you know that a healthy sign of an incredible prayer life is when you pray for things that don't necessarily benefit you? You might be amazed by how deeply the answer touches *you*, just as the answer to Jeanette's prayer for another touched her own heart.

— Ask God to give you a burden for a particular nation or ethnic group.

— Pray for those you're going to serve or those that God is going to bring you in contact with so you can tell them about Christ.

— Make a list of things you can pray for that are unselfish and have nothing to do with blessing your life:

1. _____

2. _____

3. _____

NOW IT'S your TURN!

In the preceding pages you've read true stories of teens who were rescued from drugs, pornography, violence, and broken families; how God came in the midst of everyday problems like loneliness, rejection, and discouragement; and how He can change a high school and a family through the prayers of one person or a small group. You've also seen from the lives of the young men and women in this book that regardless of where you are in your life or what you're going through, God is ready and waiting to embrace you, wrap you in His loving arms, and guide you into the future and hope He has planned for you. His love for you is out of this world! It's a forever-love, and you can come to Him right now, wherever you are.

God wants you to draw near to Him, and as you do, His

promise is that He will draw near to you (see James 4:8)! He wants you to pray so you'll know Him better and better and so He can bless your life, guide you now and all through your journey on earth, and impact the world through *your* prayers.

God's power is amazing—the mightiest force in the universe—and it will be released just as it was in the lives of these teens when *you* pray.

Now it's your turn to take the strategies in the "God Links" and the inspiration and hope you've gained and unleash a storm of prayer on your campus, in your family, and in the world. As you pray, "May [God] grant you your heart's desire and fulfill all your plans. May there be shouts of joy when we hear the news of your victory, flags flying with praise to God for all that he has done for you. May he answer all your prayers!" (Psalm 20:4–5, TLB).

**If you have a story about how God
worked when you prayed,
we'd love for you to e-mail us at
prayer@whenwepray.com
or
cheri@cherifuller.com**

about the authors

Cheri Fuller is an inspirational speaker and the award-winning author of more than twenty-eight books, including *When Mothers Pray, When Couples Pray, The Fragrance of Kindness: Giving the Gift of Encouragement*, and others.

With a master's degree in English Literature, Cheri writes magazine articles, and books that provide encouragement to people throughout the U.S. and other countries.

Cheri is founder of Families Pray USA, whose purpose is to equip and encourage parents, teens, children, and churches to impact their world through prayer, and she has a heart for youth and a desire to see true revival spring up in their generation.

Cheri frequently speaks at conferences and retreats and has been a guest on hundreds of radio programs such as *Focus on the Family,* Moody's *Prime Time America, Parent Talk, NBC Radio News,* and others. She's a contributing editor for *Today's Christian Woman* and serves on the editorial board of *Pray!* magazine. Cheri's Internet site, www.cherifuller.com, includes stories, resources, and creative ideas on prayer and building families. Cheri and her husband, Holmes, have three grown and married children, four grandchildren, and live in Oklahoma.

To contact Cheri for speaking engagements:

Speak Up Speaker Services
(810) 982-0898 or speakupinc@aol.com
1614 Edison Shores Place · Port Huron, MI 48060-3374

Ron Luce is the founder and president of Teen Mania Ministries and the bestselling author of numerous books and teen devotionals. Born in a broken home, Luce ran away and became involved in drug and alcohol abuse before finding Jesus at the age of sixteen. He later earned a B.A. in psychology and theology at Oral Roberts University and an M.A. in counseling and psychology at the University of Tulsa. He also completed the Owner/President Management Program at Harvard Business School.

Luce currently hosts *Acquire the Fire,* a weekly television program for teenagers. He has been a guest on *Focus on the Family* and *The 700 Club,* and he appears live in front of 250,000 teens annually at Acquire the Fire conferences. Luce has traveled to more than fifty countries, proclaiming the gospel of Jesus Christ. His dream is to empower young people to take a stand for Christ in their schools and in the world.

Ron and his wife, Katie, have three children—Hannah, Charity, and Cameron—and live in Garden Valley, Texas.

The publisher and author would love to hear your comments about this book. *Please contact us at:*
www.whenwepray.com

Teen Mania Ministries has a passion to see teens reach their world with the life-changing message of Jesus Christ. If you would like more information on Teen Mania Ministries, please fill out the information below and mail this page to:

TEEN MANIA MINISTRIES
P.O. BOX 2000
GARDEN VALLEY, TX 75771

Name _____ Age _____

Address _____

City _____ State _____

Zip _____ Country _____

Phone _____

Email _____

Please send me information about:

❑ **Global Expeditions—**
Thousands of young people are changing the world as they travel to over thirty different locations across the world.

❑ **Acquire the Fire Youth Conventions—**Teen Mania hosts weekly youth conventions across North America where teens learn how to live radically for Christ.

❑ **Xtreme Youth Camps—**
Located in Garden Valley, Texas, Teen Mania brings an extreme experience to hundreds of young people all summer long.

❑ **The Honor Academy—**Each year, high school graduates live on the Teen Mania campus in Garden Valley, Texas, for an exciting one-year program to learn faith, leadership, purpose, vision, integrity, and honor.

You can check us out on the web at www.teenmania.com or call **1-800-299-TEEN** for more information.

You can use a prayer journal in many different ways—basically there's no wrong way to journal about your prayer life. Use this journal in whatever way works best for you.

Here are some ideas: You can list praises and prayer needs for your campus, family, friends, and church and then update requests when the Lord answers. You can also use this prayer journal to actually write out your prayers—sometimes putting them on paper can make your prayers come alive in a new way. The ways in which you can journal are limitless—let the Lord lead you, and be prepared to grow in your prayer life.

Call upon the Lord as you journal. I guarantee that your efforts will be abundantly blessed. And you will see how God works...when teens pray.

My Prayer Journal

this journal belongs to:

_____

_____

date begun

_____

date ended